EXTREME
Project Manager Makeover!

Copyright © 2008 Pattie Vargas

ISBN 978-1-60145-576-5

All rights reserved. No part of this publication may be reproduced, stored in a retrieval system, or transmitted in any form or by any means, electronic, mechanical, recording or otherwise, without the prior written permission of the author.

Printed in the United States of America.

Booklocker.com, Inc.
2008

EXTREME
Project Manager Makeover!

Pattie Vargas

To Tony, Steve, Emmy, Joel and Bekah - the first and most important team in my heart!

ACKNOWLEDGEMENTS

Whoever said writing a book was easy never wrote one. I remember thinking I would dash this little missive off in a couple months, shoot it off to the publisher and eagerly start the next one. Uh....no, I don't think so. Oh, there will be another book one day – just like there was child number 2 and child number 3 – you sort of forget how hard it was in between times! I'm happy to be finished, but I am also *happy I wrote it*. I hope it inspires other project managers (and managers in general!) to be better at what they do. I know *my* job was a lot easier once I realized how much I needed the team to get things done!

There are so many people I want to acknowledge but since this isn't the Academy Awards, I'll keep it simple. Abundant thanks to:

- My colleagues at San Diego PMI who do so much to bring honor and class to the profession!
- My editors: Jen Rey and the ever-diligent, ever conscientious Rosi Weisser!
- Peter Murphey, cartoonist, extraordinaire! (http://www.murphproductions.com)
- My writer friends who shared tips, hints and encouragement (especially you, Karen!)
- The teams I managed over the years for endless amounts of material!
- My clients who pay me to do what I love!
- My family who matters more than anything in the whole world!

Table of Contents

FROM THE AUTHOR: WHY EXTREME PROJECT MANAGERS?............ XI

CHAPTER ONE: WHY NOW?..1

CHAPTER TWO: WHAT'S IT GONNA TAKE AND WILL IT HURT?..................15

CHAPTER THREE: ASSUME THE POSITION (THE POSITION OF LEADER, THAT IS!)............29

CHAPTER FOUR: INVEST IN TEAM DEVELOPMENT – AND *WE'RE NOT TALKING MONEY!*............51

CHAPTER FIVE: CAN'T WE ALL JUST GET ALONG?............69

CHAPTER SIX: DON'T BLAME ME! (OR, OH, NO, NOT THAT ACCOUNTABILITY THING AGAIN!)......81

CHAPTER SEVEN: I'LL KNOW IT WHEN I SEE IT!......97

APPENDIX 101

    FUN (AT LEAST *I* THINK SO!) ACTIVITIES............102

    OUTRAGEOUS MOTIVATORS............110

IT'S NOT THE MONEY!............117

ABOUT PATTIE VARGAS............119

From the Author: Why Extreme Project Managers?

It was bound to happen.

First there was **Extreme Makeover – the Body Edition.** The producers of the show searched for perfectly normal, average looking people and convinced them they would be happier, sexier, richer and produce brighter children if they only *looked* a little better. So they whittled away a little here, added a little (or a lot!) there, plumped up, slimmed down, colored, cut and styled, producing a group of contestants who looked *nothing* like they did at the start of the program! Then they chose a winner based on some arbitrary measurement process. Usually the winner, in their newly reincarnated form, was someone none of us would want to be caught *dead* with for fear of looking really bad! Then someone might say to us, "Hey, there's this TV show you should really look into …"

Next came **Extreme Makeover, the Home Edition**. A better premise – at least there was a needy family who would benefit from the home improvements performed by the Design Team, a group of young people with more heart than taste, as evidenced by some of the resulting rooms … ok, I really do *love* this TV show and it is guaranteed to be a 3-hanky night whenever I watch. But come on, sometimes it does go a bit over the top … a bedroom designed like a tree house, complete with swinging vines? I spent most of my time trying to *keep* the kids from jumping off the furniture, not *encouraging* it!

In keeping with the Extreme theme, in the technology industry we embarked on what was called **Extreme Programming**. Software engineers used to spend endless hours in analysis and design, gathering requirements from their customers, writing design specifications and building prototypes before ever actually creating the final product. It took a lot of time, but it usually (I say usually!) guaranteed the finished deliverable was pretty close to what the customer ordered. In an effort to speed things up, we just took out all the analysis and documentation and got right to programming. The final result was delivered much quicker but introduced a new competency requirement – that of convincing the customer that what you *built* is really what they *wanted* all along. (I know you wanted a toaster but look how cool this go-cart is!)

So is it any wonder that all of these *extreme* changes required that those managing them should go *extreme*, as well? And yet, while the world was morphing at the speed of light, many of us in the project management profession continued with business as usual; maintaining our GANTT charts, managing scope, crying over decreased budgets and disappearing sponsors … busier than we'd ever been. And just as predictably, project success seemed to always be just outside our reach. Even when we managed to meet a majority of the deliverables and close the project out close to on time and nearly within budget, we knew there was one success criteria we hadn't achieved – and that involved *the team*. Too often we found we put the interpersonal relationships on a back burner in favor of other priorities. After all, satisfying the customer and our sponsor was the most important thing, right? **Absolutely!**

But was it possible that:
- we could have actually performed *better*?
- the *quality* of our deliverable could have been improved?
- we missed opportunities to discover *a more creative and effective approach* to the solution?
- You, as the project manager, could have been more *influential and effective*?
- we might have finished the project and still *liked one another* rather than counting the days until this ordeal was over????

The time has come – we need an **Extreme Project Manager Makeover!**

It isn't going to hurt, nothing will get cut off, glued on, and the final result will come closer to what the customer ordered than ever before. And you just might find you start enjoying your job a little more ... I can guarantee that *those you lead* will!

Chapter One: Why Now?

It's a New Job with New Job Requirements!
Project Managers are being called upon to do more than ever before – and often, in today's economy, with less! Consider this actual job posting from a well-known job board:

Wanted: Project Manager
Minimum Requirements:
- Manage, lead and motivate highly skilled project teams
- Motivate a varied, cross-functional staff
- Lead and promote change, growth and effectiveness
- Forge collaborative relationships among cross-functional teams

Must possess:
- Proven leadership of technical and non-technical teams
- Exceptional collaborative, teaming and consensus building abilities
- Proficiency in staff motivation, conflict resolution and disciplinary procedures
- Experience in staff management, recruitment and selection, creation of goals and objectives, performance assessment

Notice some very interesting things about this posting. *Nowhere does it say anything about technical project management skills.* It doesn't mention certifications or credentials. It doesn't specify the project tracking software that is used. Why? Because the company that posted this position assumes those are a given – if you are an experienced project manager, you should possess those skills already. They will be able to discern this from your resume.

But clearly, what this company has discovered – and probably after much pain – they need an **Extreme** Project Manager! The EPM realizes that his or her technical prowess will only take them so far. How many times is the word *motivate* used in the description above? I don't know about you, but I've never been particularly *motivated* by someone's resume. Impressed maybe, but motivated...naaah. Your credentials or experience may initially lend some credibility but *your actions* can just as easily destroy it.

How about the word *collaborative* – that's mentioned twice! Collaboration requires that we bring diverse workgroups together and facilitate effective partnerships. Before we are able to collaborate on something, we have to share a mutual goal and display a similar commitment to reaching that goal. How do we go about that?

Finally, notice that the Project Manager this organization is looking for is a leader. And not just a *project* leader, a *people* leader.

Clearly, Toto, we're not in Kansas anymore.

It's a New Workplace!
In case you've been asleep for the last decade, the workplace itself has undergone quite the metamorphosis. It *looks* different in terms of gender, culture, ethnicity and

generational variables. To a lesser extent, it *acts* different as organizations react to the changing demographics. Be patient, it takes time to turn a behemoth around. And structurally, the workplace is adapting in order to compete more effectively. Let's begin by examining some of those different structures.

Organizational Structure 101

My graduate degree is in Organizational Management so this is a subject I have studied and written about extensively. But when they handed out our textbooks and they looked strangely like an *Etch-A-Sketch*, I should have had a clue. It seemed that just as quickly as we identified a structure, it either disappeared, reinvented itself or some new and improved one took its place! This gave new meaning to the term*"...seemed like a good idea at the time..."*

For the sake of brevity, let's stick with the tried and true – call them whatever new buzzword you like:

The Functional Organization

This structure has been the standard for most organizations for centuries. It looks like a pyramid with all the little people placed somewhere in that pyramid depending on who they report to. This is referred to as *hierarchy*. The closer you get to the top, the fewer people there are, the fancier the title, the more slippery the slope and the thinner the air. Project Managers who work in this organization have been well schooled to understand that they have very little authority, even less power and have to fight it out with functional managers to have resources assigned to the project. Some companies have gone so far as to install mud-wrestling pits in their parking lot just to even out the odds. (Ok, I made that part up, but maybe it's not such a bad idea - it might have actually improved my chances!)

The Matrix Organization

This is an interesting one. Many organizations claim to have a Matrix structure but it is curious that Matrix is broken down into two types: *Weak* Matrix and *Strong* Matrix. Everyone will claim theirs is a Strong Matrix. After all, who wants to be viewed as a weakling? But the proof is in the mud-wrestling pit. The premise in a Strong Matrix is that cross-functional resources are pulled from departments across the organization and assigned to projects that are critical to achieving strategic company goals. The Project Manager over these important projects wields an immense amount of power and authority over those resources. However, strategic plans tend to get lost in the day-to-day crises and the Strong Matrix can turn into a Weak Matrix with one phone call from the Vice-President of Squeaky Wheels. Just like that, the functional manager reclaims his resource and the hapless Project Manager is left with a schedule that didn't change, a list of deliverables that actually grew and fewer people with which to do it!

The Projectized Organization

Now, I've heard of this phenomenon. It ranks up there with the Loch Ness Monster – I know it exists somewhere but I've never actually seen it. The PMBOK® Guide (*A Guide to the Project Management Body of Knowledge*) defines the Projectized Organization as: *Any organizational structure in which the project manager has full authority to assign priorities, apply resources, and direct the work of persons assigned to the project.* Sounds like the Strong Matrix but obviously giving it a new name puts a little meat on the bones. To take the concept further, resources are often co-located, but it isn't necessary. One so-called projectized structure that I worked in had two team members in Europe, with the rest of us in the States. I made a strong case for co-locating all of us to Belgium but no one went for it. So much for their commitment to being Projectized. Geez – go figure.

All kidding aside, this would be a great model to work within. All of the resources are allocated as needed to accomplish the goals of the project. When one project completes, they go back into the pool ready for the next assignment. The company has systems in place that track costs and resources efficiently and the Project Manager has both the authority and responsibility to manage all parts of the project. In this type of structure the need for being an Extreme Project Manager becomes even greater! After all, if you have all this power and authority, you have little excuse - it stands to reason you should be able to deliver. And in the window of time allotted to that project, you need to get those plug-and-play resources *on your side fast!*

Regardless of the organizational structure, it is highly likely that your project will consist of cross-functional resources. In chapter three, we will discuss how to build influence and extract peak performance from individuals who do not report directly to you. When faced with conflicting priorities, your project success depends on ensuring that your deliverables have as high a weight in their minds as those assigned by their immediate supervisor.

The Workplace Goulash

My mom used to make a meal called goulash. Not Hungarian Goulash – just goulash. What it really meant was "The day before grocery day was time to clean-out all the leftovers." She mixed it all together and, amazingly, it tasted really good. The result was actually greater than the sum of the parts!

So it is in our multi-cultural, multi-generational, multi-ethnic workplace. The more diverse, the better the ideas. New perspectives. Greater imagination. Provided, of course, that the project manager doesn't apply a one-size-fits-all management style to those on the team and expect *them* to adjust to *you*. **What?** But I'm the Project Manager! You just said I'm a workplace leader! Exactly, Weed-hopper. To be a great leader requires that you have someone to lead. And the best way to lose your audience is to treat them as a blob instead of as individuals. We'll get to more of that later.

Let's consider just the *generational* diversity among our teams, as evidenced by a recent Workplace Study:
- Young boomers – those born at the tail end of the baby boom – held an average of 10.2 jobs between the ages of 18 and 38. And those jobs were not necessarily within the same company, as an expected result of upward movement. Not only did they switch companies, they changed careers, looking for more interesting opportunities! The *work*

they do and *who they do it with* had a big impact on those decisions.
- Less than 28% of the workplace today is made up of those between the ages of 30-40 years old. Many of them have instead elected to start and run their own companies, exercising more control over what they work on.
- Many retirees are re-entering the workplace as they find themselves sandwiched between the care of elder parents and the support of adult children and the ensuing financial responsibilities of it all.
- Gen X, Y have grown up in the era of corporate and political misbehavior. They are less likely to respect you simply because you are in charge – you'll have to *earn* their respect and loyalty.

The recognition that we need a "work/life balance" has become widespread and many people are actually beginning to believe it. This can spell disaster for an unrealistic schedule! This was brought home to me one day while talking to my oldest son, Steve. He casually informed me that he and "some of the guys" were going snowboarding the next day. I was aghast! The conversation went something like this:

> *Self-righteous me:* "You can't go snowboarding tomorrow!"
> *Steve, the puzzled young worker:* "Why?"
> *Me:* "Because it's a Wednesday! You can't go snowboarding on a Wednesday!"
> *Steve, the enlightened, young worker, looking at me with pity:* "I have tons of vacation hours on the books. We're going snowboarding!"

This mindset is having a contagious effect on *all* of the generations as we scratch our heads and ask, "Huh – I guess he's right. Why don't *I* start using some of those vacation hours I keep losing every year???"

How about the retention issue? According to Marcus Buckingham, leading expert on employee retention and productivity, the single greatest reason for leaving, cited on employee exit surveys, is a poor relationship with the immediate manager or supervisor. And before you tell yourself this isn't that big of a deal consider these statistics from Nancy Ahlrichs, human resources consultant and author:
- 67% of all employees are looking for a job on some level; 56% actively plan to change employers within the next 3 years.
- 1 in 11 technology employees left their organizations in 2004 – up 30% from 2003.
- 75% of *top* employees feel confident in their ability to easily find another job.

Can your project afford a revolving door like that?

Communication, Anyone?
Call them soft skills, people skills, whatever – I prefer to call them *Relational Skills*. As the configurations of our projects continue to change and the less control we have over the makeup of the teams, the more important these relational skills become. In fact, investment in the development of those skills is a *practical business decision with a tremendous ROI*. Let's look at communication modalities, for example. Experts tell us that our message is communicated in three ways: our

body language, the tone of our voice, and the words that we use.

The pie chart below demonstrates the impact and weight of each:

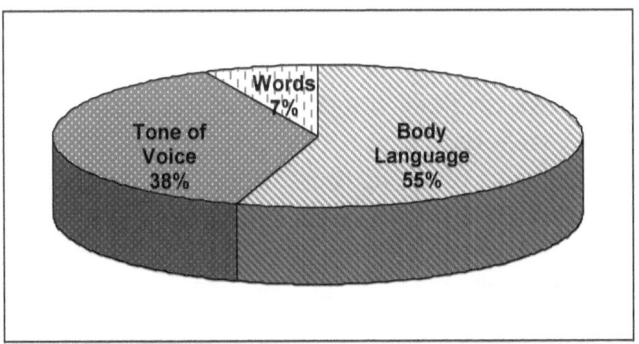

Approximately **55%** of our message is communicated by our *body language*. If I am smiling when I tell you we're going to scrap our technology for something brand-spanking new and shiny just as we are entering the implementation phase, of course, you'll know I'm joking! But if you can't see my facial expression you might swallow that cyanide capsule before I can say, "Just kidding – gotcha!"

Approximately **38%** of our message is conveyed in the *tone of voice* we use (can you say *sarcasm??*). Just think of how you can change the meaning of the phrase "Good job!" simply by changing your voice inflection!

The remaining measly **7%** of our message relies on the *actual words we use*. For those of us who consider ourselves to be quite eloquent, this is a humbling statistic!

So what's the relevance of communication modalities to managing people? It's simply one more data point to reinforce the premise that we need to be constantly evaluating the environment around us and then adjust accordingly. I personally prefer most of my communication to be done via email. It provides an audit trail and gives me a chance to evaluate a situation, prepare a response and manage the timing of my delivery. On the other hand, it also provides endless opportunities for misinterpretation and the never-ending chain of re: re: re: re: re: re: as we desperately try to clear up a misunderstanding that could have been avoided by HAVING A CONVERSATION!

In a workplace that has become increasingly diverse in terms of culture and ethnicity, the face-to-face interaction can alleviate a lot of miscommunication. In lieu of that, at least incorporating the spoken word can provide the additional interpretation of intent. If you are managing a project with a distributed work team, never rely solely on email as your mode of communication. If face-to-face meetings are not possible, conduct regular on-line meetings with teleconferencing, if not video conferencing, capabilities.

The bottom line is, it's not about how we as managers prefer to communicate. It's not about expecting our teams to adapt to our management style. It's about how we as *leaders* learn to flex and adapt to ensure the success of those we are leading. We need new tools to compete in the ever-changing workplace in order to produce quality deliverables. Consider the risk of saying the most *expensive* words in the English language: *We've always done it this way!*

Reputational Risk

One of my clients coined this term and I immediately swiped it. (Consultants are allowed – yea, encouraged – to do this. However, the rule does not apply once the stolen thought is included in that same consultant's *book*.) Project Managers are very familiar with risk – we devise complex, detailed risk assessments and contingencies to protect the integrity of the project. We consider risk in terms of resource availability, technologies chosen, budget and market conditions. All are very important to the client and to the project itself. But how about what matters to you as an individual? What about your reputation? Think of the risk to our credibility and careers if we allow a project to get away from us!

Benjamin Zander, conductor for the Boston Philharmonic orchestra, made an astounding discovery, many, many years into his career. The orchestra conductor is the only musician who *never sounds a note!* He depends on the skill and mastery of the musicians he leads for his power – for his reputation. True, it is his face on the record jackets and his name in lights on the theatre marquees. But if he can not extract from his orchestra their very best, if he is unable to persuade them to come together and deliver exquisite, top-quality musicianship, there goes his reputation.

What a wonderful metaphor for project management! I led individuals with diverse skill sets – software engineers, system and data analysts, database architects, network specialists. I possessed some (one or two, maybe) of those skills, but not all! If they were not delivering for one reason or another, I didn't have the option of jumping in and just doing it myself – I *needed* them to perform. We can threaten, cajole, intimidate those we lead into performing, but that technique is not sustainable. Fear is only effective as a motivator for a season – the minute another opportunity presents itself, the oppressed will take it in a heartbeat. For the sake of our reputations as project managers, the sooner we develop more effective means of motivation and influence, the more successful we will be.

I learned early on that of all the moving parts of a project, there were really very few that I could control. Now, follow me here, and put your PMBOK® back on the shelf for just a minute: I had little control over the budget. I was often handed a budget to begin with only to have it slashed or appropriated or otherwise manipulated by those with lengthier titles than mine.

I had limited power over the project scope. I've heard many project managers brag about their ability to manage scope. Yet when faced with pressure from the VP of Squeaky Wheels that I alluded to earlier, they cave in with the best of us. It is simply the nature of project management. (Ok, as a nod to all those project management best practices that I completely agree with, you can include these things in the risk assessment – and I would encourage you to do so – and you can implement various change control processes, but ultimately change is going to occur and impact your ability to maintain *total* control. You can join a support group for control freaks to deal with this painful truth.)

But what I *could* control was how my team interacted with one another and with me. This was one area where I could wield a tremendous amount of influence and have a powerful impact on the successful outcome of the project. When a group of individuals finally becomes a team, the odds greatly increase in your favor. Creating a cohesive, gelled unit, working in community to achieve a common goal, is the surest guarantee of success that I've found!

So what do you want to be known for? What do you want your reputation to be as a project manager? Do you measure your success by timeliness? That is one factor certainly. But you could come in on time because you skipped tasks 7, 24, 32 and 56. Within budget? Another success factor, true, but also one that doesn't tell the whole story. I've come in under budget many times but they never gave *me* any of the money I saved so whoopde-doo. Where does quality figure in as a success factor? If I had a choice, I would sacrifice budget and schedule for higher quality, but we all know that something in that triple constraint usually has to give.

Here's how I measured success in my projects:
- On time – meaning whatever deadline I negotiated with my customers and sponsors by keeping them in the loop and well apprised of any issues.
- Within budget – you usually can't go back for more so this one is important to manage well.
- Happy customers and sponsors – which spoke to the **quality** of what I delivered.
- Team members who are proud of their product, committed to the project and *ready to work for me again.*

That last one was the most important to me. If I nailed that one, I had already ensured the other three.

You see, my dear project manager, you can't do it alone. As Barbra Streisand sang decades ago ... "people who need people are the luckiest people in the world!"

Chapter Two: What's It Gonna Take and Will It Hurt?

Touchy-feely Time

Truly enlightened organizations know that good people skills will be a success differentiator in the coming years. After all, even with Extreme Automation we still need people to get things done. And the people on your projects can either work with you and on your behalf or they can just as easily sabotage your best laid plans. Lest you pooh-pooh the notion of the passive-aggressive team member, let me share an example with you.

One of my PM colleagues had a young man working for him who also happened to be the only person in the organization with expertise in a particular software program. As luck would have it, I was in need of his skill to complete one of my project deliverables. I booked a meeting with my colleague, who I will call Will – not his real name but think of *Will* in terms of *stubborn and obstinate* – you get the picture.

> *"Will, I need to ask if I can use Bob for a few weeks on the XYZ Project."* Might as well get right to the point – the less time I had to hang out with this particular fellow, the happier I would be. Will leaned back in his chair and smiled at me with a mixture of condescension and pity.
> *"If you need him for three weeks worth of work I hope you've padded your schedule,"* he warned. *"He spends most of his time dodging any real labor – lots of coffee breaks and can never make it to a meeting on time. He's yet to make a delivery date!"*

Now, this was not good news for me since I had NO pad in my schedule. In fact, I was toying with the idea of setting clocks back in everyone's office so they wouldn't know when it was quitting time. Nevertheless, I'd had a few encounters with Bob and found him to be a little quirky but pleasant enough. I decided to dig a little deeper, even though it meant spending a little more time with good, ol' Will.

> "So how do you handle him? What do you do when he's late on his deliverables?"
> Will chuckled softly and leaned over his desk, ready to share his profound management tips with me. "I always pad my schedule – for everything! I've never had <u>anyone</u> deliver on time! Bob is worse than most of them but, come on, we all know that team members are notorious for screwing up and running behind! I <u>count on them</u> being poor performers!"

Aha, I thought. No wonder. The problem isn't with Bob as much as the problem was with Will. Bob was simply responding in a pretty typical passive-aggressive way to the expectation that Will had set. I left his office with permission to schedule Bob into the plan thankful that *Will himself* had no particular skills that I needed on my project! In fact, I was pretty sure that Will *didn't have any skills that the company really needed, either!*

I contend that many employee problems are actually *management problems*. And yet, organizations spend an inordinate amount of time and energy in devising plans to deal with poor employee performance. The process improvement gene in my DNA has a real problem with this – examining the end result and wondering why it looks so bad without ever looking a little further upstream. Trying to fix an employee morale or performance issue without looking at all the inputs is like wondering why all the cars coming off the assembly line are blue when that's the only color paint being used!

Poorly managed workgroups are the key reason for low productivity and profitability. When teams have a leader (and I use the word loosely) like Will, we find projects that are completed late, or missing deliverables or of such poor quality as to ensure lack of customer satisfaction. Not so touchy-feely – we're talking bottom line impact - a direct correlation between the ability to lead and manage people well, and the profit margin.

Performance is a tangible, visible effect of a root cause. And while there may be many root causes, the ones I am going to focus on are the ones we can control – our management style and technique, and consider three indicators in particular:
- Productivity and profitability
- Team morale
- Resource Retention

As a project manager, whether your team resources report directly to you or not, it is your responsibility to engage them and gain their commitment to the collective success of the team. As mentioned earlier, and to be reiterated ad nauseaum throughout the rest of the book, the rules have changed, along with the role of the project manager as *organizational leader and change agent.*

Productivity and profitability
A Gallup survey found that, statistically speaking, poorly managed workgroups are 50% less productive and 44% less profitable than those with a clear sense of purpose and direction. Interesting that this particular citation doesn't address the behavior, talent or quality of the individual team members, but rather seems to indicate that the *management* of the workgroup might be the first place to look when identifying key causes. In my experience from both sides of the desk, I would have to agree. Obviously there are exceptions to the rule, and I will provide a caveat at the end of this section, but I have found that there were very few poor performers on my projects or in the groups I managed. Some of the contributing factors may have been:

> **Good hiring or selection processes:** Whenever possible, I involved others in the selection process, preferably those they would be working with. In addition to technical skills or talents, their ability to gel with me and the other team members was just as important. In addition, I couldn't possibly be the subject matter expert for all areas needed on the project so I deferred to those who knew better and sought their input and expertise. In the event I was not able to select the team members, I still relied on the other team members to help formulate my opinion of the individuals. This is not to say I had no opinions of my own. I just learned early on that I was not nearly as effective when operating in a vacuum.
>
> **Set clear project goals and objectives:** Individuals perform better when they understand what, when,

where and WHY. It is next to impossible to extract the very best from your team if they don't have the big picture: why this project is *important,* how it plays into the *overall strategy* of the organization, what *success* would look like and *what difference it will make* if we fail. I call this the project blueprint or roadmap – we know *where* we are going and we know *how* we are going to get there. It needs to be as clear as possible – and continue to gain clarity as the project progresses. There is no substitute for this – you cannot expect peak performance from your team if you parcel out information on a "need to know" basis.

Team Morale
Somewhere way back in my formative years, I can remember my mother saying, "_____ covers a multitude of sins." Depending on the situation, she would fill in a word – for example, when she was trying to teach me to sew (the operative word being *trying*) she would say, "Ribbon and lace covers a multitude of sins." Or in terms of southern cooking, "Breading and frying covers a multitude of sins." This does NOT apply to okra, no matter how southern you are.

As I progressed in my business career, I learned that *"Relationship* covers a multitude of sins." The relationships I build with my employees, with team members, with colleagues, vendors, business partners and so on, will go a long way to ensuring success. Basically what this means is, we are far more forgiving of one another when we know one another a little more, after we have invested time in building some level of a relationship with one another. I will discuss this more in

Chapter 4 but suffice it to say that poor morale can be the catalyst for poor project performance. If managers find themselves spending an inordinate amount of time managing conflict and putting out fires, they might want to look at the team morale and consider what they could do to improve it.

Resource Retention
Experts across the board agree that the cost of replacing workers can rise to two and a half times their annual salary, not including the indirect costs of lost knowledge, declining morale, and rising inefficiencies. Resource turnover is incredibly expensive – not only in the hard costs of recruitment, but also in the soft costs of productivity loss and downtime. Anytime you lose someone there is a gap in your project – someone isn't doing the work you allocated to that resource, someone else is picking up the slack which decreases their effectiveness. When you do finally fill the position, they have to be acclimated to the project and brought up to speed. All of this signals a hit to your schedule and, possibly, the quality of your deliverables.

So retention is a big deal – and yet employees aren't feeling the love. Very few employees today report that they see any evidence that their organizations are actively trying to retain them. In fact, according to the 2007 Spherion Emerging Workforce© Study only 13 percent are doing more to retain their employees, while, according to the employees, 29 percent are actually doing *less*. Consequently, 31 percent of employees are planning to look for a new job within the next year. This is one area, however, where you might be able to exert some influence. The number one reason for leaving a job, as evidenced by exit surveys, is a poor relationship with the immediate supervisor. I restate my position that employee performance is often a management issue. Even when an organization fails to put good retention strategies into place, the relationship with the immediate supervisor or manager can help stem the tide *for awhile*. By making sure your team likes working *for you and with one another*, you might retain them long enough to finish your project.

I can hear you now .... I'm a project manager, not the CEO of the company. I have no control over the culture of the company and, therefore, no control over retention. I strongly, vehemently, violently, categorically ... you get the picture ... disagree. You have the ability to create the *culture within the culture.* Regardless of what else is going on in the organization, people can love working for and with you and stick it out as long as they are needed. Commitment and loyalty are attainable traits.

I Didn't Pick This Team, I Inherited This Mess!
I promised you a caveat and here it is in the form of a sad story with a somewhat happy ending and a strong moral.

Many years ago I was working for a company that provided technical resources for the Help Desk industry. On my first assignment with them I was serving as Program Manager on a system implementation with oversight for three interdependent projects. There are several clues in that sentence: *first assignment, system implementation,* and *three projects.* Here's what I learned within the first three days of this project launch:

- The project kick-off had been done without me – before I was hired. During the kick-off, the scope was presented and agreed to by all parties. The scope was ridiculous – too much work, too little time, large amounts of vagueness and ambiguity.
- The project team was made up of seven Help Desk professionals. (Excuse me, I started choking on that one. After all these years I *still* can't say that with a straight face.) Here is the team breakdown:
    - Martha – No consulting experience to speak of. Worked on a Help Desk for awhile. Recently returned to the company following a leave of absence brought about by emotional instability and anger issues. The company thought a "change of scenery" would do her good.
    - John – Some consulting experience. Managed a Help Desk for awhile. Likes to talk on the phone and make deals. Good at managing up.
    - Susie – No consulting experience. No Help Desk experience. Last job was working in her mother's dry cleaning shop. Met our CEO in a bar and told him she wanted to travel. Was very, very, very, very, very attractive and "friendly".
    - Bill – Some consulting experience. Great Help Desk knowledge and ability to document policies and procedures.
    - Ivan – No consulting experience. No Help Desk experience. Last job was managing a software QA department in another country. Lived across the street from our CEO and wanted to work in the US – the CEO thought he'd make a good VP of Consulting for our company. (Get that?

OUR COMPANY. In other words, MY FUTURE BOSS.)
- Anne – No consulting experience. Managed Help Desks. Had been a customer of our company so knew what it took to satisfy a customer. Great skills.
- Oliver – No consulting experience. No Help Desk experience. New to the company. Everything about this kid was outstanding - skills, talent, attitude!

So if you were keeping score, 3 of the 7 were of no use whatsoever.

To summarize my dilemma, I had an impossible scope and a less than stellar team, and no authority to make any changes to the timeline. The third day of the job I was walking around the parking lot, thinking, fretting, wondering what I was going to do. I called my husband from my cell phone and poured out my sad tale of woe and ended up with, "This project would be so much easier if I didn't have to do it with *these people!*"

All the things that occurred during that baptism by fire could fill a book on their own, but the most valuable thing I learned was that, given all the things I couldn't control, I better learn how to manage the staff I had been handed. I learned how to 1) Identify the right issue and 2) Solve the right problem. I looked at many of the resources I had been assigned as problems. I saw their shortcomings and failures without understanding why. Once I took a different approach and spent just a short amount of time with each of them as individuals, I learned some interesting things.

Believe me, this was not easy. Staring down the gun barrel of a ridiculous schedule, taking time out to get to know the team seemed ridiculous. But it was this project that taught me how incredibly valuable this effort was and never again did I view it as "optional".

Identify the right issue and solve the right problem

Scenario One
Identify the right issue: Susie wasn't a bimbo – she simply had no experience doing what I was asking her to do. Her expectation was that I would teach her all she needed to know, while my expectation was that I had been sent an experienced professional. When I learned what her background was and how she had come to be on my job in the first place, it completely changed my point of view about her. I felt empathy for her and anger at my CEO for putting both of us in such a ridiculous position, not to mention violating the customer by expecting them to pay top consultant dollar for inexperienced personnel.
Solve the right problem: I called back to the home office, explained the situation and said I was sending Susie back for additional training and to gain experience. I declined their offer to replace her and kept my fingers crossed that no one would tell my CEO. (Remember, I was new!)

Scenario Two
Identify the right issue: I mentioned that Ivan's last job had been managing a software QA department in another country. What I didn't mention was that Ivan only showed up to my job site three times. Each time, in order to justify

his lack of deliverables, he would tell me what he *should* be working on – never what he was assigned, but what he ought to doing, *if I were a better manager*. I learned it was all a smokescreen when I was reviewing timecards and found he was claiming to be on the job when he wasn't. Further investigation turned up that he would tell the home office he was working with me and tell me he was working at the home office. Turns out he was actually still working at his old job and double dipping! (Hey - maybe he *was* suited for being the VP of Consulting!)

Solve the right problem: This one was a little easier since the home office also felt they were being duped. I sent him back to them to deal with but they ultimately dealt him right out the door. Not sure what that did for the neighborly relationships – don't care.

Scenario Three

Identify the right issue: There was an obvious integrity issue when it came to billing customers for unqualified resources. It was simply a question of ethics – I had them and the company didn't.

Solve the right problem: After a few short months, I resigned my position and went to work elsewhere.

In the first two situations mentioned above, additional training was not a solution. Neither was revising their role on the team. In Susie's circumstance, training might have turned her into a stellar performer, but it was not appropriate to do that at our customer's expense. No amount of training would turn Ivan into an accountable, trustworthy team member. As a project manager, you need to be sure to *identify the right issue and solve the right problem*. When you have done all that you **can do** or

should do to improve morale or performance, sometimes it's just a bad team fit and they need to move on. If at all possible, remove them from the team and replace them with another resource. If it is not within your power to do so, I recommend *marginalizing* them as much as possible to minimize their impact to the team. While I find the term *marginalize* to be rather disrespectful and not the way I prefer to manage my teams, there are times when it is the only appropriate thing to do.

The last scenario leads us to the moral of the story:
Never say yes to a project until you've seen the scope and know the team. When this is not possible, question the framework and foundation of the company and why they are offering you up as a sacrificial lamb. Ultimately, when all signs point to a significant integrity disconnect, pay attention. A damaged reputation is a hard thing to mend and I, for one, have enough trouble sleeping at night.

By the way – I DID deliver the scope of work within the scheduled time. It would not have been possible without the remaining members of the TEAM.

Develop Leadership Skills or Get a Really Big Stick
Having worked for all kinds of people in various types of organizations and situations, I have seen those who *drove* people and those who *led* people. I believe that differentiation is what determines how well things get done. I heard a young, inexperienced CEO say once, "My leadership style is to push people further than they think they can go." I honestly don't think he meant that the way it sounded – I think he meant that he likes to challenge

people and let them rise to the occasion. Or, who knows, maybe he really meant to just keep pushing people until they fall off into the abyss ... I know I've worked for people like that! Whatever his intent, here is the truth, and you can write it down and take it to the bank: You can push people to perform at extraordinary levels and produce amazing results. You can do this through threats, manipulation, whining, lies, fear or whatever else has worked for you in the past. You can even convince yourself that this is your *leadership style*. It will most assuredly work.

For awhile.

It is not sustainable. People will only be *pushed* as long as the vehicle you are using is viable. When the fear lessens, they will dump you faster than you can get a clue. What do I mean? When the market turns around, when organizations are hiring for their skill set, when they get a big income tax refund and can afford to take a risk and make a change....

And in the meantime, you have people working for you who resent you, hate the project, are apathetic to the goals of the organization, and quietly sabotaging any hope of success. In this dynamic, fluid business climate, I contend we don't need *more project managers* – we need more **Extreme Project Managers**. If you're up for the challenge, and I don't think you'd be reading this book if you weren't at least mildly interested, you'll need to develop new, key Leadership Competencies.

Extreme Project managers must:
- Assume a Leadership Role
- Invest in team development
- Learn to manage conflict
- Learn how to balance Empowerment with Accountability

If you don't agree, or you're not willing to invest the time and effort it's going to take to develop these characteristics, I suggest you find yourself a very large stick and carry it with you everywhere you go. You'll need it!

Chapter Three: Assume the Position
(The position of leader, that is!)

Look again at the job description we read in chapter one:

Wanted: Project Manager
Minimum Requirements:
- Manage, lead and motivate highly skilled project teams
- Motivate a varied, cross-functional staff
- Lead and promote change, growth and effectiveness
- Forge collaborative relationships among cross-functional teams

Must possess:
- Proven leadership of technical and non-technical teams
- Exceptional collaborative, teaming and consensus building abilities
- Proficiency in staff motivation, conflict resolution and disciplinary procedures
- Experience in staff management, recruitment and selection, creation of goals and objectives, performance assessment

How many of you read a description like this and want to run and hide? I don't want to manage *people,* for gosh sakes, I just want to manage *projects!* I'm a *project manager*, after all! On top of managing the schedule, watching the budget, controlling the scope, I'm supposed to add teacher, psychologist, babysitter, referee and juggler? Good grief! (You really don't want to get me started on that again, do you? Every task that needs people to complete it requires people skills – **relational skills**. There – that settles it. I don't want to hear any more whining about it.)

If we are the least bit strategic in our thinking, we really don't have a choice on whether or not to assume the leadership role. Doing so is a reasonable business decision, an added insurance factor to delivering ROI. If you're not convinced, imagine how you will deliver your project without the people assigned to it. We are aware that, in the case of a software implementation project, we cannot do without the software itself. We need the machines the software will be installed on, and we must have the infrastructure that carries the software to the end user. For a construction project, the lumber and other building materials are necessary, the blueprint of the design is a key requirement, and the equipment is needed to carry out the heavy lifting. All of these inputs are integral to performing the work and we wouldn't think of eliminating any of them – they are *immovable requirements*.

The human resources on the project are just as necessary – every bit as much a requirement for getting the job done. And, even more than the others, *immovable*. When talking about people, that word *immovable* takes on a double entendre. You cannot complete the project without them, so they can't be eliminated (immovable) and unless you manage them well, they can make sure you don't succeed by refusing to perform (immovable). We can understand why the terms people skills, interpersonal competencies, and soft skills are gaining more credibility in terms of leadership competencies. They are no longer in the nice-to-have column – they are a leading indicator of future success.

The leadership competencies for the Extreme Project Manager include:
- Be a Champion for the Team
- Develop good management skills
- Learn how to motivate others
- Build a good culture

This is certainly not an exhaustive list, but I believe these are the key elements to being a good project leader. If we are able to nail these, the rest will follow as necessary.

Be a Champion for the Team
I'm a big NBA fan so I use a lot of analogies from the game of basketball in my project management teaching and training. My favorite NBA team has struggled in recent years due to some ill-advised management decisions (I am being incredibly generous here.) The arrival of a new coach was thought to be the answer but more than halfway through the season it was clear there were more problems than could be settled by replacing the coach. My husband and I were fortunate enough to secure seats behind the bench for a recent game. I eagerly looked forward to having an up-close view of the interpersonal goings-on and maybe gain some insight to what was going wrong with my team.

Now this is a young team. There are a few veterans but the majority of the players are young and relatively inexperienced, although very talented. The first thing I noticed from our vantage point was that two of the three veterans weren't suited up – they were injured and were sitting out the game. That's fine, except that the star player's injury was not all that serious and had kept him sidelined all season. As big a fan as I am of this particular player, I honestly couldn't help wondering why – was it the coach's decision? The player's? Some renegade agent? As the game progressed I noticed that during team huddles, these two players barely managed to drag their butts off the bench to join in the discussion – not good. They both were disengaged, uninvolved, and clearly were miles away in their minds.

The remaining veteran played the majority of the game but he was *off* – missed most of his shots and didn't seem connected to the other players. We saw flashes of his prior brilliance, but overall he performed like a player who was desperate to be traded.

The younger players displayed a great deal of talent but very little teamwork. The longer I watched, the more frustrated I became – remember, I was viewing this from the floor – not five feet from the game huddles where the body language was easy to read. The message came through loud and clear – this team did not respect their coach. The next day I understood why. In an interview, the coach took *no* responsibility for the team's poor performance – instead he criticized the way *they* executed the plays *he* called and questioned the commitment of the players sitting out the game. The team did not respect their coach, because *he did not respect them.*

Here is a fundamental truth to write down and store in your memory banks forever – **talent is not enough**. You can rearrange the components a million times, trade a player, acquire four more, make all your decisions based on stats and facts – and fail, fail, fail.

Being a champion for the team means you are *one of them*. You don't see yourself as a separate entity – you, leader and them, team. Rather than operating from a position of power, the champion views him or herself as the *serving* member of the team. Stephen Covey says, "...the basic task of leadership is to increase the standard of living and quality of life for all stakeholders." Rather than being synonymous with power, leadership is actually servanthood. Picture the standard organizational chart with the "leaders" at the top and the typical boxes illustrating those beneath them - now turn that chart upside down, with the "leaders" at the bottom supporting the others and you have *Servant Leadership.* It is this very act of selflessness that inspires others to follow, and actually prevents leading from a position of manipulation – it is authentic – it is transformational. A true leader demonstrates humility and a desire to serve, operating from a place of relationship with those in the trenches. He or she believes in the vision and demonstrates a *belief in their people to implement that vision.*

The team champion would never throw the team under the bus in order to excuse himself – *they are the team*. Rather they assume responsibility for the actions and performance of the team – they certainly deal with performance issues, and we will discuss that in a minute. But they don't separate themselves from the consequences anymore than they should claim all the glory in times of success.

Being a champion for the team means you believe in the collective power of the team and you do all in your power to protect the *structural integrity* of the team. What do I mean by this? Imagine your house – and some bully comes in your home and begins kicking at a load bearing wall. They are kicking with all their might but you don't pay all that much attention because, after all, what can their puny kicking do? So they go off and come back with a sledge hammer and, while you're not paying attention, begin whacking away at that all important load bearing wall. Suddenly there's a hole, then it gets bigger, and you see the roof beginning to sag …. Before you know it, the whole thing is in danger of collapse.

Those bullies attack your project team, too. They might come in the form of a jealous co-worker who resents the project, your role on it, or any number of things. The bully may come in the guise of an organizational leader whose agenda is at odds with yours. Worse yet, it can come from within – a team member with a grudge or an axe to grind who stirs up dissention from within. Regardless of the motivation, *those bullies will come* and their goal is to destroy the structural integrity of the team – to bring down those load-bearing walls. Your job is to prevent it from happening, and we will learn more about how to do that as we progress through the book.

Just Manage Will Ya? (*Or*, Develop Good Management Skills)

For years, the trend in organizational thinking has been that leaders *lead* and managers *do*. While it is true that both roles require very different skills, the line between the two is becoming more and more blurred. In today's new organizational structure Extreme Project Managers are being compelled to the front lines, where they belong – giving instruction, providing guidance and - dare we say it - *leading* the charge.

Yes, as a leader, I believe the EPM realizes that more than a title or authority is needed; in fact, often they have very little direct authority. But while we are developing the necessary *leadership* skills, we can't neglect the importance of *management* skills.

I once worked in an organization where one of the leaders was extremely good at motivating, exciting, stirring things up. But he consistently fell flat on time-sensitive tasks like providing necessary input on reports or submitting change requests. He once allowed an entire folder of performance reviews with their associated salary increases to sit on his desk through his vacation – and past the deadline for submission. He delayed providing his input for a presentation we were co-presenting to the CEO until I was forced to write his part myself in order to make the publication deadline. Although some were willing to excuse this behavior, chalking it up to the *perceived* differences between leaders and managers, I couldn't accept this. I resented his inattention to the details that were *extremely important to me* – good leaders recognize the impact their actions have on others.

Organizations need both management and leadership – and more and more they need them to be one and the same person! Managing is a subset of leadership – the good leader must both lead and manage equally well. This is not to say that they need to possess all the qualities of a good manager and a good leader – that's rather unlikely. But what does anyone do when they lack a skill – you either *acquire* it, or you *find* it in someone else. If you as the project manager / leader are not good at managing all the day-to-day nuts and bolts tasks, then find someone in the group who is. If you can't seem to book a meeting, or sign a timecard on time, or publish the minutes, delegate! The leader should *know their own weaknesses and not be afraid to admit them* – use the strengths of others to ensure that the *needs of those we are leading are being met*. Our shortcomings should never penalize those in our charge. That's *good management*.

Managing well also means dealing with discipline and performance issues – the people side of things. We can't wish or hope away a problem and this is one instance where your mother was wrong: Ignoring something doesn't make it go away. The EPM is a good assessor of skills and talents; if they are fortunate enough to assemble the team, they use whatever tools are available to ensure the skills are adequate for the task and to ascertain whether or not the person is a good fit with the team. As mentioned earlier, I always relied on others to help make both determinations, and the *one time* I didn't was a complete disaster. I still have the scars to prove it.

If you are not able to assemble the team yourself (if you inherit the team), it is even more important to manage performance issues in an effective and timely manner. Few things are more disrespectful to your team than turning a blind eye to the poor performer and refusing to deal with a discipline issue. On one of my projects, there were two resources assigned to a large part of the work, and the skills needed were difficult to find (that was my first excuse). I had not hired either of these resources (that was my second excuse) but nevertheless I was on the hook for delivering.

As time went on, it was evident that one of the individuals assigned was not keeping up. Upon discussing it with him, I learned that he felt his skills were "a bit rusty" and he thought he would benefit from some additional training. Even though there was no room in the schedule for training and I had not counted on having to train a senior programmer on the language in which they were supposedly fluent, I felt I had no recourse but to send him to a week of training. (Ouch – it still hurts). Imagine my surprise when his performance did not improve and, during intervention discussion number two, he claimed the requirements were vague and the users dimwitted. I was not as forgiving this time since, well, *I* had written the requirements and, dimwitted or not, these were the only users we had. So I placed him on a PIP – Performance Improvement Plan for all you HR-y people, with a fixed timeline for improvement. The final straw, though, and what allowed me to kick this person off the project with absolute glee rather than feeling sorry for him, was the extra added burden his poor performance placed on the other, highly skilled, uber-dedicated engineer.

Motivate Me!
Old school management techniques were simple. The boss told employees what to do and they did it. Adherence to authority was key and "because I said so" was a completely acceptable reason. But business today is dynamic, with the need for speedy innovation and constant change being standard operating procedure. In such an environment, employees must be "managed" differently – rather than dictating directions, today's leaders must set the course and then remove the roadblocks that would prohibit the staff from achieving it. They have to become more involved in order to motivate the troops.

Motivation – there's a loaded concept. There are millions of books written on the subject and the underlying motivation for motivating your people (that sounds a bit cyclical, doesn't it?) covers a wide range. On one end, and a concept I resent a great deal, is the idea that employees and team members are too inept or lazy to be intrinsically motivated, so you need to provide a tangible incentive. I call this the carrot and stick approach – unfortunately, subscribers to this theory are often carrying the same *really big stick* we talked about earlier in the chapter. On the other end is what I call Santa Clause management – just give them lots of toys and they'll be so ecstatic you can get them to do anything you want. I'll admit, I'm a little closer to Santa Clause than the other end, but the difference for me is in the transparency of your agenda. I'm not big on manipulation; rather I am a proponent for painting a vision, helping them see where they fit into that vision and why their performance is critical to achieving it.

Great leaders know how to paint a vision – what separates the great from the (yawn) so-so is their ability to excite and inspire others, to create loyalty to the vision and release potential and creativity that ensures top quality deliverables. This is a noble and lofty goal – it is also completely attainable by following some down-to-earth guidelines to gain team buy-in.

Step One – Forget Consensus
If we were in a movie theater and flames suddenly started shooting out from the screen, when the theater manager stood up in front and said, "Everyone needs to leave the building immediately" there would be **full consensus** that it would be wise to follow his suggestion. Beyond that, consensus is pretty much unattainable. Consensus as defined in The American Heritage Dictionary, means, *An opinion or position reached by a group as a whole.* Now, I've managed people for long enough to know that there is no such animal, except, of course, in the emergency

situation mentioned above. Just trying to decide where to go for lunch has often launched an hour long debate!

The EPM knows that, while consensus is not likely, they *can* reach **buy-in** by doing the following:
- Allow time for discussion – give the participants the opportunity to air their concerns or opinions. This creates the willingness to rally around the vision or a team decision because they know they have been heard and their thoughts considered. You can't just bring your great idea to the table, demand everyone rubber-stamp it, and expect the team to *buy-in*.
- Avoid analysis paralysis – don't allow the discussions to go on indefinitely out of fear of making a wrong decision, or the unwillingness to make the final move. This undermines the confidence of the team in you as the leader – just as deadly as not allowing their input.
- In the event that you use this process as a decision making tool, once the discussions are over, restate what decision the team has come to. This is a great way to identify that what you *thought* was crystal clear actually was – well, wasn't as clear as you thought. Be sure the direction is clear before assuming you have commitment.

Step Two – Hold them accountable to the vision
Since you've allowed open dissent and discussion, once the decision has been made, the EPM has to protect the integrity of the team by holding them individually accountable to the vision. There is a dangerous ripple effect across your organization when your team does not display a commitment to the goal. It shows up in

miscommunications – not everyone promoting the same direction - and in a lack of progress or missed milestones. These breakdowns make the entire team look bad, damages your reputation as a project manager, and undermines your influence with others.

In addition to gaining your team members' buy-in to the vision and goals, there are other practices that I have found immensely effective in motivating others:
- Develop and demonstrate good listening skills. There is nothing less motivating than knowing the other person isn't really listening to what you have to say. This falls firmly in the category of manipulation – the leader pretends they want to hear what you have to say but you know they're simply patronizing you. If you don't want input, don't ask for it. If you do, stop what you're doing and LISTEN. Take notes if you feel it's noteworthy. Open your mind to *actually consider* what the other person is saying rather than waiting for them to finish so you can paste on your plastic smile and say, "Great idea – I'll give it some thought! (NOT!)" Give yourself room to entertain the idea that you just might not be *all that and a bag of chips* and be open to input.
- Be willing to ask for help. What a relief to know you don't have to do it all alone – that there are others on your team who have skills you lack and are willing to help! This is hugely motivating and demonstrates your confidence in their ability.
- Celebrate milestones and accomplishments. Don't wait until the end of the project to reward achievement – that is too far away! Find celebratory moments along the course of the project to keep the

team engaged and involved and to alleviate stress and boredom. These celebrations don't need to cost money or – God forbid – require upper management approval. Bring cookies to the status meeting at the end of a grueling week. Publicly recognize something a team member did. Call a momentary work stoppage to hold a Chinese Fire Drill – I'll tell you more about that in the Appendix.

Ken Blanchard contends that the best leaders motivate and empower others by "letting them bring their brains to work and expecting them use their minds to solve problems and create solutions." Rather than restricting that collective brain power out of insecurity or fear, we can exponentially increase our chance of success by doing something wild and crazy like – oh, I don't know, UNLEASHING IT!

Put on Your Hard Hat and Become a Cultural Engineer (Build the Culture That Encourages Excellence)
When I teach or counsel project managers on team development, I often hear, "You don't know my company. They'd never go for that...the culture here is so bad!" The funny thing is, I've yet to find a company that didn't have *something* wrong with their culture, somewhere. Granted, some are worse than others, but here's a newsflash for you – you can create a culture within the culture! And another bit of advice – don't ask for permission! As long as you're not violating any company policies, why do you need permission to motivate your team or to do a good job? The rewards are endless and the company benefits from your success, so build away!

Inevitably the next comment will be, "I don't have any budget for that." Oh, please. I NEVER had any budget for rewards and recognition. One company I worked for used to give the managers $100.00 a year to use, at their discretion, for some kind of team celebration. One year this got cut to $50.00; we had barely finished grumbling about it when they cut it out of the budget altogether, saving a whopping $1400.00 a year. My answer to the "I can't afford it" excuse is, you can't afford NOT to. But I'm getting ahead of myself – back to the steps for building a great culture within a culture:

Step One: Develop the Necessary Traits for a Cultural Engineer

- **Honesty:** Be honest with yourself, with your team, with your sponsor and with your customer. Don't have one story you tell your sponsor and another that you tell your customer – granted, you need to tailor the message to the hearer, but don't LIE. You will get caught when you forget who you told what.
- **Humility:** Assemble team members who are smarter than you are – each member adds a strategic component that increases the probability of success. If you're the smartest person on your team, you're in trouble.
- **Willingness to take a risk with your people:** Take a chance – tap into the collective talent of the individuals on your team by considering their past efforts and lessons learned.
- **Take responsibility:** When things go wrong, don't look around for someone else to blame. You're the leader – take the hit. On the other hand, don't be a patsy either – deal with incompetence or performance

issues on the team. If there are outside circumstances that could pose a negative influence on the project outcome, escalate those issues in a timely manner. Don't "take the hit" when something is outside your control – manage it appropriately.

- **Be a Relationship Builder** - This one is a two-parter:
  - ***Build Collaborative Relationships:*** Your ability to build strong collaborative relationships with cross-functional workgroups, customers, sponsors, vendors, etc, etc, etc. will make things so much easier for your team. Refusing to do so just makes their job that much harder. It is your job as an EPM to forge the way for them and remove roadblocks where necessary. I'm sure you are well aware that, in all organizations, there's the way things are done and then *there's the way things are done.* Your job is to find out what *that other way* is and work well within that process. Let me give you an example:

    I managed a software development team that was chartered with developing the systems and applications that were used internally. Our products were not glamorous like the commercial products, they were functional, like payroll systems and financial accounting – yes, not glamorous but certainly necessary! To move a product into production was a lengthy process with many approval gates. If we were in line with too many commercial products, ours would inevitably be pushed to the end of the line since our "customers" were only internal – a mindset I did not agree with, obviously, but that's how it was.

Over time I developed a good rapport with the "gate keepers" - those who made the schedule, gave approvals and moved the process along. It wasn't manipulation, it was good business. Plus, it's just more enjoyable to work in a collaborative vs. adversarial manner with your co-workers. Our team even instituted a Thanksgiving ritual where we made huge platters of goodies and treats and delivered them to those gatekeepers to acknowledge their contribution to our success. The end result? We seldom got pushed to the end of the line – they enjoyed working with us, it was mutually respectful and beneficial – and we were able to keep to a schedule.

- **Build Relationships with Your People:** Maybe you subscribe to the "Me, Boss … You, Peon" mentality. If so, I have to say, "How's that workin' for ya?" We all spend way too much time on the job and I've found that the better the relationship, the higher the quality of the deliverable. Everyone has things going on – we are all multi-dimensional with interests, problems and situations. You don't have to be best friends with your team members – in fact, that's not a good idea. But you can have a healthy, friendly relationship with each of them without violating any kind of company policy or unwritten laws of nature. When you have a better understanding of the individuals on your team, you can apply a more holistic style of management – one that takes into consideration the whole person, not just the resource assigned to your project. It pays off in the long run – and it also allows them to see you in a different light, as well. We are far more likely to be more forgiving and accommodating of one another when we allow ourselves to see some of that human element in one another.

Step Two: Validate, Validate, and then Validate some more!
There is no such thing as over-validation. I've yet to hear anyone say, *"Boy I wish the company would stop giving us those bonuses when we come in under budget!"* Ok, maybe that doesn't happen in your company but I've also never heard anyone say, *"Don't acknowledge my hard work."* Truett Cathay, founder of Chik-Fil-A, had a saying: "Who needs encouragement? Everyone." Truer words were never spoken. Engineers need praise. Analysts need praise. Doctors, lawyers, teachers, kids, husbands, wives, waiters need praise. We all need the encouragement we get when someone recognizes our efforts and accomplishments. Granted, it's a good idea to take into account the personalities involved and praise them accordingly – your shy employee may not appreciate being called up on stage in front of the company – but everyone appreciates the acknowledgement.

The EPM makes validation and recognition a part of the team culture. It doesn't matter if the organization has such practices – we're talking about building a culture of excellence where your team will flourish and succeed. Never miss an opportunity to show your appreciation not only for effort and accomplishment, but also for *loyalty and consistency*. And do it often. You'll find a list of ideas to meet every need and budget in the Appendix – feel free to steal them from me, that's why they're there!

Alas, a caveat...
I'm not a Pollyanna. I've worked for some great companies and I've worked for some that I could have sworn were Portals to the Gates of Hell. I firmly believe you can create the culture you want for your team, regardless of the organization's culture .... but it won't be eternally sustainable. Ultimately you as a leader will come to the place where you simply can't stem the tide any longer. When your successes are becoming few and far between, and you are spending more time fighting the bureaucracy than getting anything meaningful accomplished, it's time to pack it in and look for the next great opportunity. Maintain a good relationship with those around you and encourage your team members to pay attention to their careers and do what's right for themselves, too. Leave on good terms and don't look back.

Authenticity – Not Just Lip Service
All of the information dispensed in this chapter is valuable and, in my humble opinion, necessary to being an Extreme Project Manager. But we've all seen the "leader" who learns about the latest great idea and implements it because that's what they *think* they should do. The lesson never leaves their head and works it's way down into their hearts so their actions, while appropriate, never ring true.

The United States Army follows a leadership theory known as "Be, Know, Do." It is very simple in its foundational meaning, which is what I believe makes it so profound. The U.S. Army defines leadership as "influencing people by providing purpose, direction and motivation, while operating to accomplish the mission and improving the organization." The very premise of that purpose statement is that you must have, on your team, motivated people with a clear understanding of the mission in order to accomplish the goals of the organization. Otherwise, the leader yells "Charge!" and storms up the hill, only to look back and find he's standing there alone, exposed and vulnerable to the enemy.

When it comes to management, I liken the "Be, Know, Do" theory to this:

Be: Your Character
Know: Your Competence
Do: Your Actions

Self-evaluation of the first tenet, your character, can lead to a more honest assessment of the second tenet, your competence, as well as your limitations. I recommend that managers take a few minutes to go deep within and try to understand their own motivations and identify the values that are the most important to them, that go toward shaping their character. Mark Sanborn, author of the brilliant little book, The Fred Factor, said, "Integrity is the distance between your lips and your life." Aligning your *actions* with your *character* is what ensures your authenticity. No one wants to follow a hypocrite.

EXTREME Project Manager Makeover!

You may have done this exercise before, but it bears repeating. Find a quiet place of solitude and don't rush this time of introspection, but don't over think it, either. Usually the first thing that comes to mind is the most accurate.

Values, Principles and Beliefs

Circle the 15-20 values, principles or beliefs that you feel are the most important to you.

Achievement	Family	Joy	Resiliency
Affection	Financial Security	Justice	Respect
Affiliation	Forgiveness	Leadership	Responsibility
Ambition	Freedom	Learning	Self-Control
Authority	Friendship	Logic	Self-reliance
Autonomy	Fun	Love	Self-respect
Belonging	God	Loyalty	Service
Caring	Generosity	Make a Difference	Sincerity
Challenge	Genuineness	Money	Spirituality
Companionship	Happiness	Nature	Stability
Control	Health	Obedience	Status
Courage	Helpfulness	Order	Success
Dependability	Honesty	Peace	Taking Risks
Discipline	Independence	Power	Teamwork
Dignity	Integrity	Pride	Tenderness
Effectiveness	Intellect	Purpose	Tranquility
Ethics	Involvement	Recognition	Wealth
Equality	Imagination	Reliable	Winning
Fame	Initiative	Religion	Wisdom

Of the items circled above, list the 5 values that you feel are the most important to you.

_____
_____
_____
_____
_____

The five values listed above help identify your motivators and define your character. By gaining clarity in this dimension, managers can ensure that their actions are in alignment and demonstrate their commitment to maintaining that character. For example, if one of your top 5 was *equality* and yet you find yourself not treating your team members in an equal and fair manner, all your platitudes about valuing the team won't be believed. Conversely, if winning was on that top 5 list, you might want to increase your awareness so you can recognize when *your need to win* impacts your relationships with the members of your team.

If the job description from Chapter One is accurate and we are requiring leadership competencies in our project managers, nothing we've discussed so far is optional. It takes discipline, integrity and self-awareness to motivate others and build effective relationships. And as I mentioned earlier in this chapter, assuming that leadership role is *a reasonable business decision*, an added insurance factor to delivering ROI.

Chapter Four – Invest in Team Development – and *we're not talking money!*

Have I mentioned yet that the people on your team are your most valued asset and, as such, deserve the highest percentage of your time and attention? Well, in case you've missed that point, it's true. All of the resources used to successfully complete your project are important, but the *human* resources are the ones who can talk back, provide support, quit, deliver exceptional quality, sabotage you – well, you get the idea. It is imperative that you develop your team – a wise investment of your time and energy. Occasionally you may need to spend some money for training, rewards or recruitment, but, by far, the biggest investment will be of yourself.

This doesn't always come naturally to us. Some people are, by nature, team builders – they thrive on collaboration and partnership and just seem to have the ability to "rally the troops". Others wonder why we can't all just do our jobs and deliver top-notch work without having to engage in – God forbid – conversations or other interactions. My experience in managing teams is that, regardless of the various personalities and behavioral styles involved, just about everyone appreciated being involved in more than just their little piece of the project. The quality of their deliverable was greatly improved by having a greater understanding of the overall goal. In fact, if they *didn't* want to know, it was cause for concern as it raised a red flag, at least to me, on the level of their commitment to the team and the organization.

Consider this quote by Robert Levit, PHd. and Campus Chair for University College at University of Phoenix, Jersey City, NJ: "Humans do not perform at peak performance unless you engage them as humans. If you want peak productivity and peak customer service, *you must engage the human spirit, the sense of meaningfulness* in what they are doing." There is nothing more disrespectful than telling an employee or team member to just "sit down, shut up, and do what you're told." And yet, that is exactly what we do when we don't paint a clear picture of what the goals and objectives of the project are – when we assume they either don't want to know, or they don't *need* to know.

Extreme Project Managers invest a great deal in team development because they know it is the only real way to gain the commitment of those they lead. Because it is *not optional* that you learn how to do this, I've broken it down into some basic building blocks for you to learn and put to use.

Step One: Understand the team composition
You do not have widgets assigned to your project – you have people. People with personalities and motivators and funny little quirks. The sooner you recognize what those are, the more quickly you can develop a strategy for either using those differences or putting plans in place to mitigate them. I recommend two methods for understanding your team make-up:
    1. DISC Behavioral Assessments: Originally developed in the 1920's by William Moulton Marston, the behavioral theory behind DISC has gone through various modifications resulting in the DISC Behavioral

Assessment used today to identify the 15 classical patterns of behavior within these four dimensions: Dominant, Interactive, Steady and Compliant. Although there are many different assessment tools, among them Myers-Briggs, Kolbe, Personality Skills Inventory, and others, I find the DISC assessment easy for my clients to use and understand. I particularly like the implementation model used by Dr. Tony Allessandra that stresses the importance of taking what we learn about ourselves and then applying it to *improving our interactions with others*. Called **The Platinum Rule**, Dr. Allessandra encourages participants to recognize the style trait of another and then treat that person as *they* would like to be treated, not how *we* would like to be treated. When taking a style inventory or behavioral assessment, we often focus inward on our own make-up and how we behave, how we like to be treated. The real benefit comes in creating an awareness around the styles of others and understanding why we find it so easy to get along with some people, while we struggle in our interactions with others. With that understanding, we can develop communication strategies to use with the different styles.

So what does DISC mean? First, DISC is a *style* assessment, not a *skill* assessment. There is no right or wrong way to be – you cannot flunk your DISC test! We all have some of each type - your DISC profile is based on a combination of these four primary dimensions:

Dominant (or Dominant Director):
- Like to call the shots for themselves and direct others
- Prefer challenging workloads which fuel their energy level
- Speak their mind, often without forethought
- Enjoy taking risks and being involved in changes
- Prefer to interpret the rules and answer only to themselves

Interactive (or Interactive Socializer)
- Like to work participatively with others
- Need immediate feedback
- Seek friendly, stimulating, favorable environments
- Enjoy compliments about themselves and their accomplishments
- Are motivated by quickly attainable goals; tend to lose interest over time
- Prefer verbal or demonstrated instruction and guidance

Steady (or Steady Relater)
- Dislike taking risks or "change for change sake"
- Enjoy working in a stable, steady, low-key environment with minimal "drama"
- Like to know each logical step toward completing a task – begin with the end in mind
- Prefer to make decisions with the group or other processes, rather than by themselves
- Enjoy feeling they are a valued member of the team

Compliant (or Cautious Thinkers – think *Compliance*)
- Prefer to set and maintain the quality control standards

- Like to work with systems and data and prefer to build them themselves
- Workplaces that are organized and process-oriented, with minimal socializing
- Superiors who value their focus on correctness and let them know their importance to the organization
- The flexibility to invent or design their own method or model
- Dislike change or surprise and will view it as poor planning

You may be surprised at the make-up of the people on your team – depending on the kind of project you may find a majority of the members fall into a similar make-up. This is not surprising as different professions attract different kinds of styles. For example, I often find that on teams that are in a service or support function, we will see a higher percentage of Steady Relaters and Cautious Thinkers. These individuals are usually good at working on a team to resolve technical or complex issues and recognize the need to provide quality support and problem resolution. However, they can sometimes become stuck in the minutiae – and spend too much time trying to find *exactly the right answer* – good enough is not in their vocabulary. This team could benefit from a Dominant Director who is able to make decisions and move the action forward.

Then there are those fun, lively, imaginative marketing teams where we often find a lot of Interacting Socializers and a sprinkling of Dominant Directors. They have great ideas and can generate a killer product description in four color, full-bleed layout, complete with a deadline for going to market, only to have a Steady Relater or Cautious Thinker ruin it for them by mentioning that what they envision is *not even remotely possible in the timeframe they have promised.*

Do you see how the teams we lead could be, without better understanding, one big playground fight just waiting to happen? By using the DISC assessment, or any other one for that matter, we can head off misunderstandings and bad blood by recognizing that we all have our own make-up and not all styles will interact as effectively with one another as with others. It prevents disagreements from becoming personal or attaching malevolent intent to miscommunication or simple misunderstandings.

If at all possible, have your team members complete a DISC Assessment and discuss the findings as a team. Depending on the provider, there are options available at all price ranges – contact me if you'd like more information.

2. The good, ol' "Meet and Greet": I've heard many project managers dismiss this as a "touchy-feely" waste of time. Au contraire! If I could cut anything out of the project launch meeting, it would be the time we waste waiting on those Really Important People who can't seem to get to a meeting on time*, but NEVER the Meet and Greet.

What's the Meet and Greet? It's when you go around the table and everyone gives their name and background. Depending on the type of project or organizational structure, there are other things you may want to know – skill sets, their assigned role, or other information. Some project managers include a kind of ice-breaker question - "Tell us something no one would guess about you" – but this could be awkward in the first meeting; use your best judgment. Even when the project team is meeting virtually, the meet and greet ritual is very beneficial. You will learn a lot more about your team than simply the information that they share. For example, you can gauge who is "into" the exercise and who resents it. That can be an early clue as to their level of interest in the project or their perception of their own self-importance. You might get a sense of how the members interact with one another and if there is any "bad blood" among some members or possibly any "cliques".

If the team is meeting virtually, ask the members to submit this information to you ahead of time, post it on the electronic whiteboard and then go ahead and conduct the exercise while on line or on the phone together. Even though you may not all be able to see one another's faces, you can gauge involvement by how quickly they comply and return the information to you, as well as by the verbal interactions.

I strongly recommend using both methods, DISC and the Meet and Greet, to gain a better understanding of the composition of your team. If you are unable to do both, be sure to do the latter. The more you understand about those you are leading, the more strategic you can be in your efforts.

(*Never wait on people who can't get to your meeting on time. Regardless of their stature, start the meeting on time, smile sweetly when they meander in, and continue. If they ask about something that has already been discussed, politely tell them you'll catch them up after the meeting. You, as the lowly PM can afford to waste your time in retelling a story to rude people, but you can't afford to have your resources sit through it again. If the meeting cannot begin because the tardy person is a required attendee, wait no longer than 10 minutes, then reschedule the meeting. As you can probably tell, this is a major bone of contention for me. And before you write me on this topic, I know, I know, I know, I know, I know, I know that there are exceptions to every rule. But if I ruled the world, this one would have NO exceptions.)

Step Two: Establish the Basic Ground Rules
Oh, come on, surely we are beyond that. Well, evidently not, at least based on what my past experience has been in managing projects. And while I don't agree with those who start each and every meeting (yawn!) by rehashing the agreed upon rules and guidelines, I certainly endorse the practice of establishing them at the onset. I even recommend documenting them and publishing them somewhere – on a poster in your "war room", as an addendum in your project plan, tattooed to offenders' foreheads, you get the idea.

Your organization may already have a documented Code of Conduct or something similar, but do not count on that being known or generally accepted. If there is one, and you think it goes far enough to meet your needs, dust it off and bring it to the meeting to see if everyone else agrees. Your ground rules need to be established early on, if not at the project kick-off, then soon after. And, by the way, YOU as the PM cannot make these up and then decree them like Moses coming down from the mountain. The team needs to create the rules together, so they'll all buy-in to adhering to them. Here are some questions and topics to discuss to help identify those things that are important to your team:

- Confidentiality – what should remain confidential, i.e. customer or proprietary information?
- Professionalism – what does that mean to our team? How do we behave professionally with one another? Do we care about dress code or the team reputation outside of the room? Who will handle what roles on the team?
- Behavior – different from professionalism – this could mean the way we *act* in the meetings. How important is punctuality, the way we speak to or interact with one another?
- Expectations –How will we handle missed deadlines or poor quality or performance?

This is not an exhaustive list of topics to consider but it should get you thinking. What matters on one team may not matter to another simply because of the composition of the team, the type of project or the length of time involved. Do not neglect the act of formulating ground rules – even if this team has worked together many times before, reiterate their application.

Step Three: Be sure everyone knows the project goals
This is a big one – never assume everyone already knows or "gets it". Putting a bunch of people together in a conference room *doesn't make them a team* anymore than me standing in the middle of my garage *makes me a Subaru*. A large part of turning all those plug and play parts into a cohesive unit is being sure they know and understand the project's goals and objectives. It's naïve to think that those working on your project have the slightest clue what the company's overarching strategic goals are; but until you are able to link the project's goals to the organizational strategy, you'll have a hard time convincing them of the importance of success over failure!

In your kick-off meeting, go over the goals of the project, describe each one and discuss what they actually mean. And there can't be a hundred of them – there should only be a handful of actual goals – beyond that you're either getting into discussing deliverables or possibly into sub-projects. Use a whiteboard or some other visual means of connecting the dots: if Operational Excellence is one of the organization's goals for this year, demonstrate how this project goal ties into meeting that objective. It could be that your project addresses several corporate objectives – if so, make that linkage clear.

You will increase the commitment of your team when *they understand why* it is important in the grand scheme of things that they accomplish their mission and what the price of falling short would be.

Step Four: Maintain an Environment that Breeds Trust
Everything I have written to this point goes towards creating an environment that breeds trust between you and the team members. Trust is a funny thing – it can take a long time to develop and be lost in an instant. You can't buy it at the store and implement Trust 3.7 like quick-fix software – you have to begin with 1.0 and build from there. The EPM who assumes the role of the leader and invests their time and energy into strengthening the team has laid the foundation for trust –but it is just that – a foundation. Without proper care and feeding, it can begin to degrade until there's nothing there to sustain the weight of all that comes against the team.

Imagine carefully building a rope bridge across a treacherous canyon with raging white water rapids and jagged rocks below. You stand back, admire your handiwork, take a few brave steps out over the chasm – even tentatively jump up and down a couple of times - and then walk away, secure in the belief that what you have built will last forever.

But will it? Rope and wood won't last forever, no matter how strong it was in the beginning or how talented your workmanship. The sun beats down on your mission critical bridge, the wind and rains buffet it about, animals and other people take advantage of what you've so carefully provided, but you don't notice. You're off attending meetings, updating schedules, gathering new requirements – all in a day's work. Until one day, you arrive at the bridge, with an urgent need to get to the other side – a time when you really, really, really need this bridge to perform – only to find that more than half the planks are missing and it's attached by a single, fraying thread. Horrified, your mouth hangs open while you watch that one, little strand stretch – stretch – stretch – and then – PING! – snaps and the bridge falls away, eliminating your ability to get from HERE to THERE.

That's exactly what happens with trust. We invest a great deal of effort in the beginning to get all the team members on the same page and pulling in the same direction and when we like what we see, we turn our attention elsewhere. While we're not looking, sinister little trust-killers creep in and begin hacking away at that foundation, things like:
- Violating the team's ground rules – applying a double standard.
- Playing favorites.
- Not allowing team dissent or asking their opinion.
- Throwing the team under the bus to sponsors or management.
- Gossip, deceptive actions, hidden agendas, disrespect, all around Total Jerk Behavior.

Now, depending on the situation, the trust could be lost gradually over time, or it could be destroyed with one single whack of the axe. Regardless, once trust is lost you won't be able to reestablish it as quickly the second time. There is some fundamental law of quantum physics or something there – let's call it **The Vargas Rule of Trust Eradication and Restoration**. Sounds impressive, at least – I wonder if I can get a patent on that? But I digress … Suffice it to say, trust is the foundation of all great teamwork and without it, you'll never operate at full capacity. Pay attention and you won't be caught with your "bridges" down!

No Laughing at Work!
It's so simple, it's ridiculous – along with letting people bring their brains to work, we should let them bring their funny bones, too. I'm not sure where the notion got started that we can't have fun at work – if I have to spend more than a few hours *anywhere* you better throw in a joke or two. The cure for apathy, boredom and burnout is JOYOUS Teamwork! Yes, I said, Joyous! Ok, I hear you now, "You don't know my workplace." Do I *really* have to go there again?

One of my favorite business stories is that of Pike Place Fish Market in Seattle, Washington. Pike Place is a state-of-the-art, pristine environment with wall-to-wall carpeting, climate control, piped in classical music …. Not! It's a cold, smelly, damp FISH MARKET, for crying out loud. But what was it about that place that caused John Christensen, author of the best-selling book, FISH! to call home to co-author, Stephen Lundin, and proclaim, "This place **ROCKS** with energy!" It was the joyous, raucous teamwork that literally permeated the place!

The FISH tenets, or Mission Statement if you will, are simple:
- **Choose Your Attitude** – As one of the "fish guys" put it, "Who are you being while you're doing what you're doing? Are you bored and impatient or are you being world famous?"

- **Play** – The fish guys have fun while they work and it shows! Furthermore, it's energizing and contagious!
- **Make Their Day** – The fish guys include the customers, and one another, in their good time.
- **Be Present** – The fish guys are fully present at work. When talking to a customer, that customer has their undivided attention.

Before implementing this workplace strategy, Pike Place struggled with the same issues facing all organizations – customer retention, employee turnover, declining profits and so forth. If interjecting a little levity into their business strategy – in fact, using workplace fun as one of the *key* strategies - could work for a fish market, think what it could do for our teams!

I did my best to make the workplace as enjoyable as possible and I believe it was often the difference between

despair and hope – of just giving in to apathy or deciding to make a go of it one more day. If that sounds melodramatic to you, well, sometimes my teams were facing some steep, uphill battles. On occasion I would walk the halls and literally feel the oppression. Maybe they'd heard a rumor that the project was going to be cut or a customer had lashed out at them in frustration. Perhaps they'd had an unpleasant encounter with a team member or someone from a cross-functional business unit. Maybe they were deep in the details of a particularly difficult piece of their work that they just couldn't seem to solve. Other times it was simply that we had gone far too long without a good laugh!

Before you insist that having fun takes away from the seriousness of the job at hand, consider some of these quotes:

> "There may be 50 ways to leave your lover, but there's only 4 ways out of this airplane." Herb Kelleher, Southwest Airlines. Now as someone who flies a great deal, I think flying is serious business. But I'd rather have a happy pilot at the controls than some bitter, old sourpuss who hates his or her job!

> "There are just too many people walking around work with tight underwear!" Ken Blanchard, Ken Blanchard Companies. I've *seen* those people, and so have you, and now you know why they act like they do!

"Don't take yourself so $@!& seriously!" Benjamin Zander, Boston Philharmonic Orchestra. Coercing an orchestra to play skillfully and flawlessly requires a great deal of hard work and attention. But if you do so at the expense of the sheer joy of playing the music, what's the point?

Breaking up the tedium, stress and monotony with a little fun is a guaranteed performance enhancer and a way to foster trust and camaraderie. I modeled it for my teams, and they in turn modeled it to their customers, peers and back to me! Later on in the book you will find examples of our outrageous antics, and as I mentioned earlier, feel free to steal them and use them! But I'll share one quick story with you:

On a team I managed many years ago, there was a team member who I'll call Rhonda because that's her name. In the spirit of workplace levity and fun, Rhonda brought a "giggle ball" to work, a furry, white ball about the size of a softball with a silly face painted on it. When you threw the ball through the air, it would "giggle", although we all agreed it sounded more like a turkey gobbling, leading us to rename the "giggle ball" the "gobble ball".

Budget time was a particularly stressful time for me. The process went something like this:

1. I would work exhaustively on a budget, including everything I could possibly think of so I wouldn't have to go back for more later on, while attempting to keep it within 3-5% of the previous year's budget. The proposal included mountains of

supporting documentation so that every objection could be clearly addressed. I would submit it several days ahead of the deadline, cross my fingers and hold my breath.
2. The Keepers of the Overall Corporate Budget would return my budget, usually with only 4 hours left before the deadline with the ambiguous directive to "cut it by 5-6% without eliminating any deliverables". I soon grew wise to this tactic so, even though they were ridiculously late in making the request, I had a contingency plan in place and submitted Budget B – the REAL one, with the additional cuts in place.
3. With 30 minutes to deadline, I would receive one of those URGENT, RED-FLAG emails demanding that I cut yet another 5% and get it back to them immediately as they were preparing the budget package for the board of directors. And no, none of the project deliverables could be dropped.

My peer managers and I went through this year after year – no contingency plan ever worked, leading one of the managers to wail, "Why don't they just give me a number and I'll build a budget around it?" Silly rabbit, that would make too much sense!

So during one of these crazy budget times I had, evidently, been ignoring my team and remaining head down at my desk, probably with storm clouds growing increasingly black over my office. Suddenly, through the open door, an object whizzed past my head, "gobbling" all the while, and hit the window behind me with a loud SMACK! Startled, I looked up in alarm and saw several of my staff members peering around the corner, looking at me with cautious trepidation. It was so bizarre and incongruous that it cracked me up. The more I laughed, the harder I laughed – I couldn't stop and neither could they – they made my day and I was ever so grateful!

Chapter Five – Can't We All Just Get Along?

Conflict – just the very word conjures up thoughts of angry words, upset stomachs, maybe even throwing punches. My thesaurus suggests some very strong comparable words: clash, battle, struggle, even WAR. With such emotion involved, is it any wonder that most of us prefer to avoid conflict at any cost?

Extreme Project Managers have learned how to manage conflict – how to prepare for the inevitable as well as how to harness the positive energy that comes with disagreements. In the previous chapter, we learned how to recognize the personalities and other variables among our team members, and for good reason. We're not all the same – and, therefore, we won't always agree on methodologies, techniques or approaches. What keeps those differences from becoming a prolonged struggle depends on the skill of the project manager and the commitment of the individuals to the team.

First we should clear up some common misconceptions about conflict. This is not an all-encompassing list by any means, but just a few that I have run across both as a project manager and in my consulting practice.

1. **Harmony is normal, and conflict is abnormal.**
   In my humble opinion, nothing could be further from the truth. Now I do not personally like arguments, especially when voices are raised. But I have learned to resist the urge to rush in and play peacemaker because too often I shortchanged the brainstorming or problem resolution process.

As mentioned earlier, we are all different. Duh. Some of us talk louder when we get excited or agitated. Some of us wave our arms, or make jokes, or get very quiet. The point is, if we feel a decision is important, someone's probably not going to get their way – it's inevitable that some buttons are going to get pushed. This is especially true when the team is very invested in a successful outcome and their goal is commitment, not consensus. The EPM welcomes open debate in order to reach that place of buy-in so, guess what, not every opinion shared is going to be popular!

If you want a bunch of automatons who rubber stamp every decision you make, maybe you should consider a career as the dictator of a third world country. Great teams are made up of great people with disparate views and ideas. The EPM should be more concerned when it gets very, very quiet, *peaceful and harmonious* because it's *just not normal*. More than likely one of the following has occurred:

- One or more members of the team have been allowed to overpower too many brainstorming sessions and everyone else has just given up and let them have their way. Good for the opinion bullies, bad for the team and the customer. You need to regain control of the meetings to ensure all the opinions are heard, not just the loud ones.
- The organizational climate has become stressful and politicized and everyone is laying low out of fear. This is a hard one – you

still have a project to deliver and you need the team to perform. The solution is to build that "culture within the culture" mentioned in Chapter Three that protects the team from the noise outside. Only you can determine when that's no longer possible in your particular situation.
- You as the PM have indicated you're not interested in anyone's opinion so they're not going to give it. You've created an environment where no one is going to tell you the truth, no matter what. Go back to the beginning of this book and start again. Do not pass Go, certainly do not collect $200 and be prepared to apologize to your team members. Get serious about your role in creating a stellar team.

2. **Conflict and anger are the same thing.**
   Conflict involves emotion; anger is just one of the emotions that may be displayed. It might be the most visible or the easiest to identify, but it is not the only one that could come into play. In the face of conflict, some individuals become fearful – afraid of the possible outcome, of the strong feelings that are evident. Others withdraw or refuse to engage, appearing apathetic about the whole thing. Still others joke their way through what they perceive to be an uncomfortable situation.

   When teams disagree, it's possible that strong opinions may be voiced. Depending on the importance of the decision, it may take some time to work through those issues to ensure that the best possible solution is identified. It's important to separate *passion* from *anger*. Extreme Project Managers should jump for joy when their team members display passion for the project goals – when they care enough to engage in lively, passionate debate about how to achieve them. Productive, effective conflict is the best possible way to reach the best possible solution in the shortest amount of time.

3. **Conflict is a result of personality problems.**
Referring to conflict as a personality issue supposes that if we could all simply be more mature, the conflict would not exist. Granted, sometimes a personality problem can result in conflict, but the converse is not true. Two people can have widely diverse personalities, so disparate that they would never think to socialize with one another, and yet be completely aligned in their commitment to the project. The depth of their commitment can lead to conflict related to decisions made on that project. The conflict arises out of the differences in the way they will approach a task, or the methodology the team will use, not out of their different personalities.

4. **Conflict bad; *disagreement* good.**
Ok, now you're just splitting hairs. This one is all about *semantics* designed to help those who just can't get over that word *conflict*. So, if it

makes you feel any better, use the politically correct word, *disagreement*, although it does somewhat indicate that you didn't believe any of the previous paragraphs.

If you have attended more than one or two meetings in your time, you have likely heard someone use the phrase, "Take it off line." If the discussion that is occurring is one of those side-bar events, relevant only to the two people having the discussion, then this is a perfectly acceptable thing to do. If, on the other hand, those words are uttered by a timid project manager who has not learned how to harness the creative passion of their team, this is a cop-out. I learned early on in my career of managing teams that too often I would become uncomfortable with the passion during a debate or discussion and quickly rush to try to calm everyone down. I would become the official "shusher", trying to soothe the ruffled feathers and make all the bad stuff go away. Without meaning to, I completely short-circuited the process. Teams that argue are not wasting time, they are *saving it*. As stated earlier in this chapter, productive, effective conflict is the **best possible way** to reach the **best possible solution** in the **shortest amount of time.** Working through those hard discussions, letting the creativity take its course takes time. The problem is, avoiding the conflict *takes longer*.

So now that we know what conflict is *not*, how do we know when we are experiencing good conflict? There are some key predictors.
Conflict is ok when it is:
- Productive: The disagreement or opposing viewpoints surround topics that need to be

addressed. On a priority level, the topic is something that should be resolved in order to maintain focus, schedule, direction and so forth. The EPM can help steer the discussions to be sure they remain on point and are a good use of the team's time.

- Limited to ideas, concepts, methods: We're not arguing about the scope of the project, the relevance of the work or any other point outside the control of the project team.
- Not focused on personalities or individuals: Arguments that come about because people do not like one another have no place in your project meetings. This is a classic place where the, "Take it off-line" comment is appropriate and you may have to "take it off-line" with HR if you are unable to get these team members to set aside their personal differences for the good of the project. You can recognize that a disagreement has become personal when they begin to attack one another's character, intention, qualifications and so forth.
- Focused on the current issue and not past, residual resentments: You will recognize deviation when the team members begin to say things like, "You always" or "This is just like the time when you ..." You might also see this when a team member hasn't gotten over a past disappointment on a prior project so they continue to bring it up and liken the current issue to the past. Recognize when it's appropriate to learn from the past and when you need to cut off the negative baggage.

You can minimize the impact and disruption of conflict if you simply acknowledge that it is going to occur. You can do that by preparing for it ahead of time. You as the PM should lead the team through an exercise where you set the ground rules for handling conflict and agree to what acceptable behavior is. Your list might include the following:

- Face to face – not behind backs
- Focus on behavior and events, not personal attacks
- One problem at a time – not a litany of past misdeeds
- Allow everyone to talk – no interruptions
- Check the attitude and body language at the door
- Emphasize where you do agree – remind one another of the goals and purpose
- Acknowledge where you don't agree – sometimes restating the opinion clarifies that there is a *misunderstanding*, not a *disagreement*
- When does it need to be escalated OUTSIDE the team (last resort)
- APOLOGIZE

That last one is a biggie. Max De Pree said, "Without forgiveness, there can be no real freedom to act within a group." I have seen extremely polarizing situations diffused when one member simply stuck out their hand and said, "I apologize. Let's move forward."

Encouraging your team to develop flexibility and adaptability in dealing with one another will ensure they have more successful interactions. The more committed they are to the success of the project and the cohesiveness of the team, the more natural the tendency to flex. You might want to include the following graphic as part of your documented Ground Rules:

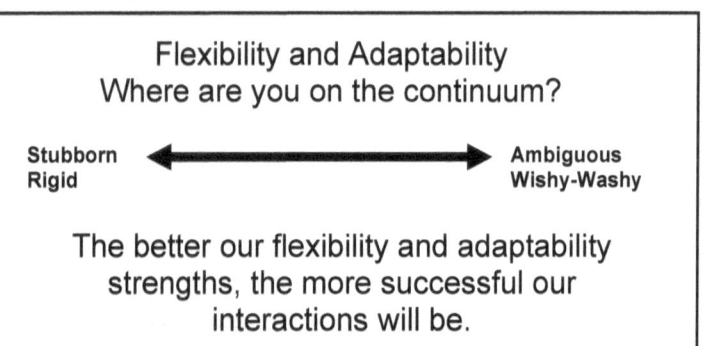

Teams that engage in effective conflict:
- Have lively, interesting meetings: The meetings aren't quiet and polite; they are somewhat volatile and energetic!
- Extract the best ideas of all team members: When open debate is encouraged, more ideas will be generated. The EPM should manage this process to ensure all team members have the opportunity to be heard.
- Solve real problems quickly: The problems are addressed during the meeting and not in the hallways or cubicles *after* the meeting.
- Minimize politics: When we are unable to effectively debate and reach decisions during our team meetings, they are often made in those hallway meetings mentioned above. They might be made between the PM and the VP of Squeaky Wheels without the benefit of exploiting the best ideas of the team.

- Aren't afraid to put critical or sensitive issues on the table for discussion: When trust is high among the team we aren't afraid to touch those touchy topics – in fact, we think too highly of one another *not* to.

So the children are fighting – what do I do?
It's likely going to occur so you might as well have a few strategies for dealing with it. As mentioned earlier, at the beginning of the project, lead the team in an exercise where you define your ground rules and agree to adhere to them.

In addition to that, consider these two indicators and your strategy for dealing with each:

- Unrest / Dissatisfaction = Unmet Needs: Maybe you've dropped a ball somewhere. Maybe you're not communicating as regularly as you should so the goals and objectives of the project are getting cloudy. Perhaps you're not protecting the team like you should from the noise and politics outside. It could be that your milestones are too far apart so the team is getting weary of never finishing anything or getting any recognition.

Assess how long it has been since you debriefed the team, not just *them* providing *you* with status. Share what you can with them about changes in organizational direction; ensure they remain apprised of how their work relates to achieving the organization's goals. Review the project schedule to see where you might break up some of the milestones or identify key delivery points in order to show progress toward the goal.

- Long time, no laugh: Throwing a party is the answer to so many things, especially in response to conflict. It is difficult to be angry with someone you just shared a good time with. Removing the team from the day-to-day grind can also reestablish lines of communication or allow your team to acknowledge areas where they are struggling with one another.

A few years ago I was managing a large, cross-functional project to integrate several applications. One of the sub-teams was made up of four individuals – all talented and necessary to the project – but with very different personalities. We would have team meetings where they were all very polite to one another, but following the meeting I would find two of them furtively whispering over in a cubicle. I'd turn the corner and find the other two, equally secretive and engrossed in their own conversation. It was obvious that the two factions were diametrically opposed in their approach to getting the work done as evidenced by the fact that no work was getting done. (They don't call me smart for nothing!) Replacing any of them on the team was not an option so something had to be done.

I called a team meeting to be held at Dave and Buster's, a local restaurant and video arcade establishment. We had a nice lunch where we talked a little about the project, while I'm sure they were all wondering what in the world we were doing there. After awhile I got up to leave and gave them their assignment: they were to stay there for the rest of the afternoon – they couldn't leave before 4pm. First order of business was to have some fun with one another and they had to mix it up, not just play with the counterpart they were the most comfortable with. I gave them some money for tokens and gained their assurance that they would play some games together. The second order of business was to sit down together and hammer out a game plan for how they would get along with each other moving forward. Mind you, they were never *fighting* – they just weren't working together. The conflict between them didn't manifest itself in anger, it showed up as gossip and polarization. They needed a set of ground rules for how they would address their disagreements so they could function as a team. And I made it clear to them that if they didn't come up with a plan, *I would*, and they might not like it.

The next morning, on my desk, was a list of agreements they had developed. Now the members of that team never became good friends, and I didn't expect them to. But I did expect them to work effectively together and deliver the work that needed to be done. By taking them out of their element and forcing them to relate to one another as more than just team members, it introduced an element of humanity to the equation and they were able to find some common meeting ground.

It takes a lot of creativity on the part of the EPM – that's what separates you from your mediocre counterparts. It means being aware of what is going on – and what's *not* going on – and intervening where necessary. Creating an environment where your team feels safe enough to engage in positive conflict doesn't leave a lot of room for politics and building coalitions pitting some team members against others. Alliances only work on Survivor – where teamwork is definitely *not* the name of the game. You don't want your team members focused on *outplaying, outwitting and outlasting* one another.

Chapter Six – Don't Blame Me! (or, Oh, No, Not That Accountability Thing Again!)

In an issue of PMNetwork magazine, a survey reported that 68% of project managers reported a problem with accountability. I could have told you that *without* a survey, as I'm sure any project manager could. Why is accountability such a difficult team attribute to achieve? I believe that accountability and empowerment go hand in hand – but it is crucial that we understand what each term really means and how both are necessary in the proper balance for success.

In recent years, accountability has gotten a bad reputation due to the rise in documented examples of corporate malfeasance of the Enron variety. Accountability has become synonymous with blame – who is responsible for this mess? Who did this? I worked for an executive who used to routinely round up all the usual suspects and demand, "Who is accountable for this?" while pounding on the table with his fist. What he meant, of course, was, "Who am I going to punish for this? Who's getting written up? *Who's getting fired?*" In that environment, there were very few of us who were willing to step up and take the hit. Accountability does not mean blame, rather it means holding something in such high regard that you will do anything and everything in your power to hold up your end of things. It would never enter your mind to slack off or perform at less than top quality and potentially damage a successful outcome. The team is everything – you're working together in group accountability – you have one another's back. It is the highest demonstration of selflessness you will ever see in the corporate world.

When a team is demonstrating group accountability, it is the surest guarantee of success you will ever have. This is *positive peer pressure* – the standards are high, the expectations are clear, and no one wants to be the one that causes the team to fail. Team accountability eliminates the need for bureaucratic punitive practices and makes your job as the PM that much easier, providing, of course, that you are holding yourself accountable, too. More about that later.

Accountable teams:
- Feel comfortable in questioning one another's activities
- Apply positive pressure on poor performers
- Enjoy mutual respect and strong partnerships
- Avoid the bureaucracy of corrective action and performance management

If you cringe just a little at any of the above, we need to talk about what accountability looks like and why you need to pay attention to how visible it is on your team.

- Teams that are comfortable in questioning one another's activities are demonstrating that they have moved beyond competition and insecurity. I'm not talking about turning on a hot, white light and saying, "Where were you the night of January 15th when that server went down?" I am referring to open and honest inquiry – "why are you working on Task 15 when we haven't completed 6-10" – that is rooted in team performance. The person inquiring is not *accusing*, and the person being questioned is not *defensive*. The question itself assumes that *one of us* needs to be enlightened or educated and it *just might be me.* If anyone on the team feels that a member is spending their time unwisely or there is a need for their time and energy elsewhere, this is the opportunity to bring it up.

- When teams are operating at a level of top performance, that alone applies positive peer pressure. It is very difficult for a poor performer to hide out in a very functional team, where achieving the goals are paramount. Extreme teams will have the "difficult conversation" – the one we usually avoid for fear of damaging the relationship. In reality, avoiding the conversation is sure to damage that relationship and all the others around it. Superficial conversations are expensive – for us as individuals, for the project, and for the organization. Tiptoeing around an issue just ensures it's going to come around again and again and again until we deal with it. Managing conflict and holding ourselves accountable are very closely linked.
- Extreme teams enjoy the camaraderie and ease that comes from sharing a common goal and sharing the same level of commitment to the result – there is a mutual respect that just gets things done. The issues of competition and jockeying for position are all settled and in the past. Members readily partner and collaborate on solutions and respectfully debate in order to achieve optimum results.
- Accountability to the team goals means we commit to meeting the expectations of the team – that if certain standards have been set, we live up to and uphold those. In addition to meeting the

deliverables, adhering to those standards are just as important. This is a wonderful example of positive peer pressure – we do not want to be the one who causes the team to fail – or cause our team member to look bad. Peer-to-peer accountability is a critical success factor on teams – it shows that the unwillingness to let another team member down motivates us more than any fear of authoritative punishment. We don't rely on bureaucratic, punitive actions to solve our problems. Things get done – we move through issues so much quicker.

I'm OK. You, I'm Not So Sure About
As you should expect by now, I have some ideas and suggestions for reinforcing team accountability. I have implemented all of these at one time or another, always with satisfactory results. In my consulting practice, when I find a reticence on the part of my customer to follow through with tangible actions, it usually indicates a lack of commitment to actually *achieving* accountability. After all, once we start putting some teeth into a concept, we might start being – oh, no! – held accountable!

True story, one of my early consulting gigs was for a group of managers who had heard me speak about team accountability at a conference. During our planning discussions, they cited "lack of accountability" as their number one problem on their internal development projects. I put together a training program with a strong emphasis on ways to reinforce accountability and obtained the support and buy-in of the management team – or so I thought.

When I arrived on site the day of the training session, I was surprised and dismayed to discover that none of these managers planned to attend the training. For a company that claimed to be concerned about "accountability" I just assumed they would participate in the process, and you know what happens when we *assume* .....yes. Basically, they wanted *me* to fix *their* people. As the day went on, it became crystal clear to me why these project teams had no accountability – they were not held to any timelines, budgets, milestones or quality standards. The company enjoyed a healthy profit line – as one attendee put it, "We are awash in cash!" and projects just went on and on and on. Everyone was getting paid and it didn't matter if they finished things or not.

Their contributions to the project were not part of the annual performance review and the project manager had no input during that process. Several of my suggestions that had been supported by the management team fell apart when the team members pushed back – in other words, no one really wanted to do anything about this. I was wasting my time and theirs.

I have since learned to refer to engagements like this as "training events". No lasting change is expected or even wanted, organizations just put on an "event" to make themselves feel better and justify their failures by blaming lack of movement on the "trainer". To avoid a lot of hassle, I think they should just mail me a check and we all stay home. So if you don't really want to address the accountability issue on your team, skip this next part and go on to the end of the book. Or better yet, just skip the rest of the book altogether – but I doubt you will. If you weren't already an Extreme Project Manager at heart, you wouldn't have gotten this far! So here we go:

- Establish an entity that's all your own – this team's. Give the team a name. One of my favorite teams to manage years ago was called Business Applications Development – yawn, how boring. We christened ourselves **BAD** and had T-shirts made that said *Another BAD Guy!*
- Come up with a short mission statement – one that is in alignment with the organization's mission. The BAD Mission Statement was: "We build and maintain business critical systems while strategically positioning Acme to maximize future business opportunities." The statement clearly expressed that we were important to the company achieving success – to staying viable – to continued growth.
- Identify some shared team values and go deeper than just the "We value collaboration" thing – what does that really mean? Be real about them. One of BAD's team values was "We expect a Can-Do Attitude". That said volumes about the level of commitment on this team.
- Here's the money shot: Develop a peer review process. Often we are measured by people who had nothing to do with the project – who weren't there in the day-to-day, nitty gritty. I always recommend to my clients that - whatever your performance review process is – you implement a peer review or team review as well. If there is no measurement, it is very hard to know how you're doing – and it is hard to institute any kind of

accountability to the team values and norms. As part of the peer review, you measure not only how the individual performed relative to their specific tasks and assignments, but also how well this team member maintained the "spirit" of the team – how they demonstrated their commitment to the overall success of the team. If the team is highly functioning, the results will usually be very favorable on all counts. You will get a more accurate view of how an individual is actually performing when their peers are involved in the process. You will also get forewarning when someone may be "going off the rails" for one reason or another. A caveat – (and don't I usually give you a caveat?):

- Involve your team in developing the peer review. They need to have clarity on how they will be measured and have a say in the process. You'll avoid a lot of hassle when an individual receives a negative review if they agreed to – and helped define – the process ahead of time.
- All team members have to be reviewed – you cannot pick and choose.
- Review with frequency – usually more often than most performance reviews. If your organization tends to hold annual reviews, conduct the peer review quarterly or possibly as part of project milestone reviews.
- Be sure the data is shared with the individual's manager if they don't report to you. It's not your problem if that manager

doesn't want or use the data, simply that the information is distributed in the same manner for all.

Let me give you two very different examples of how I saw the peer review work very effectively for two teams I managed many years ago. One of the team members was a great engineer, had the skills and abilities and his work was always top quality, but he had a hard time sticking to a schedule. After he made a couple late deliveries, we reached a milestone and conducted a peer review. His teammates praised his technical abilities but dinged him on his commitment to the schedule. The funny thing was, he honestly didn't realize that his late deliveries were holding others up. Somewhere along the way he had missed the class where they taught the concept of dependencies! I believe that having it pointed out by his peers carried a lot more weight than if I had done so – he wanted their respect and he was never late again!

Contrast that experience with another team and another team member. The project was very difficult with a lot of moving parts, a long list of tasks and an immovable schedule. If we all just kept focused on our assignments, we would be able to get it all done. To stay on schedule, we would make daily adjustments and one person would take on some of another person's tasks knowing that, in the coming days, the favor would likely be returned. The stress of such a dynamic environment apparently got to one of the individuals, though, and one day he announced he wouldn't be putting in any more overtime or assuming anyone else's tasks. The team met this announcement with incredulous stares – it was highly unusual for anyone on this team to become more focused on their own needs over the good of the group. Because of the high level of trust they shared, they felt comfortable in open debate and I was proud that the first things they wanted to know was if he was ok – if his family was ok. They were giving him the benefit of the doubt – surely he couldn't be making such a stand just because he was self-centered and selfish. But as he dug in his heels and began arguing about the merits of the project and complaining about his workload, their patience quickly began to wear thin. *Everyone* was tired. *All of us* were carrying a heavy workload, but there was an end in sight as long as we all just kept on keeping on! He would not be persuaded – this was all about him. He let the team down – others had to fill in the gap he left – and he paid the price at peer review time. He permanently damaged his relationships with the team and lost their respect. He isolated himself, losing that sense of belonging and the camaraderie that comes with everyone hanging together to accomplish a difficult job – he couldn't participate in that. When the project ended, he elected not to attend the victory party. I didn't select him for the next project and, the last I had heard, he finally left the company when other project managers continually passed him over, too.

It is not the job of the project manager to enforce accountability – it is not the team leader's job or the VP's job. It is your job. My job. Everyone's job. An accountable team is self-directed in terms of the accountability lending the direction. However it *is* the job of the project manager to *model* accountability. One of my clients had an epiphany during one of my workshops. She suddenly realized how her reticence to deal with the poor performance of one or two team members demonstrated her lack of accountability to the rest of the team. Where she had excused her behavior by calling it "kind" or "tactful", she was penalizing the team and being an impediment to their success.

A member on one of my teams was an absolutely brilliant engineer. He was one of those true geeks who lived, ate, slept and breathed new technology. He thrived in times of rapid change and innovation. I hired him to work on a new project we were launching that required a cutting-edge technology for which we did not yet have the necessary skill set. During our roundtable sessions, the project leads would give a quick status of their projects, and it was clear that he thought his project was the most important one in the pipeline and demonstrated a visible disdain for the projects that used older technologies. The first couple of times he made witty disparaging remarks I ignored him. After all, that's what my mother taught me to do with bullies. But I noticed that the other leads were becoming increasingly annoyed and realized that we were soon headed for a damaged work relationship. Since we were all very busy, I frankly didn't have time for those kinds of problems.

So the next time he made such a comment I replied, "You know, those "old" systems process your paycheck – you might want to be careful!" He laughed, along with the rest of the group, and I thought that would be the end of that. Well, it wasn't. At the very next review meeting, he made yet another wisecrack. *Brilliant*, yes. *Smart,* no. I looked him in the eye and very pointedly said something like this, "If you make one more crack like that, I will pull you off your super cool project and assign you to one of the "old" projects. You will stay there until you learn respect for your team mates." You could have heard a pin drop in the room. Now, I usually recommend that you deal with individuals one-on-one but in this instance, the team needed to see me stand up for *them*. His disrespect had been public and his reprimand needed to be as well. And

it worked – he never made such comments again. He became a respected, valued and *well-liked* member, fully committed to the spirit of the team. I'd hire him again in a heart beat. Building peer-to-peer accountability among the team – and modeling it back to them as the project manager - helps develop that attitude of commitment to one another and increases the likelihood of success.

Actions Speak Louder Than Words

I mentioned earlier that accountability and empowerment go hand in hand. A lot of managers – and companies, for that matter – give a lot of lip service to empowerment but it's really just an excuse for not holding anyone accountable. Empowering others *does not mean abdicating your responsibility to lead and direct others.* A project manager may say they believe in empowering the team to do whatever it takes to get the job done, but what they *really* mean is they don't want to be bothered with measurements or attending to detail.

Empowerment by its very definition demonstrates *your complete confidence in the team to deliver.* I would not leave a five-year old in charge of dismantling a nuclear bomb – no amount of flowery empowerment statements or motivational posters on the wall will equip them to handle that job! I could not walk away in confidence - that's not empowerment, its stupidity or worse, laziness!

Your confidence should be tangible and demonstrated by actions that empower:
- Collaboration – seeking the input and advice of the team. This accelerates knowledge sharing and affirms their skills, knowledge and value to the team.
- Flexibility – being willing to change directions or adjust your approach based on a better, more effective idea. Your flexibility encourages innovation and creativity, which leads to better solutions.
- Unwavering support – the team knows that you won't sell them out or blame them when your neck

is on the line. When the team is sure of your support, they will return the favor and go to the line for you, when it counts.
- Distributed decision making – involving the team when creating policies or guidelines. They will be far more likely to support change when they are part of it. If possible, include them in the decision to hire or add new team members, as well. Their insights on team dynamics will be very helpful for you.
- Fairness and equity – not adhering to a double standard where some team members are clearly favored over others and allowed to get away with things no one else can.

Actions can be de-motivating as well and might include some familiar ones such as:
- Weak leadership – not stepping up and letting the project flounder
- Taking personal credit for the team's success
- Dishonesty – harboring hidden agendas
- All work and no play – try continually harping at your team about how far behind they are, how hard your job is, how many times the budget has been cut – and see just how motivated and empowered they are!

Steve Nash (yes, another NBA story, but it has been awhile since I told you one) is currently the team captain for the Phoenix Suns. He is a marvelous example of positive, empowering leadership. During a playoff game against the Los Angeles Lakers, they were behind in the series 2 to 1. With 3 seconds on the clock and the Suns behind by one point, the referee made a critical error during a play between Steve Nash and Luke Walton. The Lakers made the final shot, winning the game, but photos later showed that Walton was clearly out of bounds and the referee was caught on film, staring at the play. The team was obviously angry and bitter, and expressed their feelings vehemently. Steve Nash stood up and addressed his team saying, "Yes, it was a lousy call, and yes, we could have won that game. But we are better than this! You have 10 minutes to complain about this and then *I don't want to hear another word about it.* We are better than this and we will go out there and win the next three games and the series!" And you know what? They did! The Suns joined a small group of teams who were able to win a playoff series after losing three consecutive games. Steve held them accountable to being the best team they could be – he reminded them how powerful and talented they were – and empowered them to go out there and win!

Sign me up!
You'll be able to tell when your team feels empowered. Motivated, empowered teams exhibit a confident, can-do attitude with a palpable excitement about possibilities and challenges. They will demonstrate a collective commitment to the mission and will use possessive words like our and we.

You will see a willingness to cross-train one another and take on extra tasks when another team member is struggling with a particular problem. My favorite of all – you will see them begin to model empowerment to one another and to other teams with which they interact. They will be free with rewards and recognition for a job well done.

Finally, combining the traits of accountability and empowerment, Extreme Teams use their freedom with discretion. You will be able to trust them not to violate the privileges afforded to them because of their commitment and accountability to one another. To quote Martha Stewart, "it's a good thing!"

Chapter Seven – I'll Know It When I See It!

Welcome to the summary – where we review all the things you've learned while reading this little book. I *do* hope you have learned one or two new things or at least been reminded of things you have forgotten in the heat of the battle! Beyond just learning something new, however, I sincerely hope that you put *at least one of them* into practice – then I can feel this was not an exercise in futility!

Earlier in this book I told you how I measured success in my projects:
- On time – meaning whatever deadline I negotiated with my customers and sponsors by keeping them in the loop and well apprised of any issues.
- Within budget – you usually can't go back for more so this one is important to manage well.
- Happy customers and sponsors – which spoke to the **quality** of what I delivered.
- Team members who were proud of their product and ***ready to work for me again.***

That's my success criteria – yours might be different. The good news is, we get to define our success. Yes, we have the objectives of the project, the timeline, the deliverables, but we can define the success criteria within the confines of the requirements – and point to a *higher level of achievement*. For me, that was that third bullet item – team members who were proud of what they had accomplished, were able to wrap up the project with their team relationships intact and wanted to work with me again! That higher level of achievement is what made it all worthwhile.

Extreme Project Managers have added four new competencies to their toolkit:
- Leader: Organizations today are not just looking for project leaders, they are looking for people leaders; those who don't just *drive* performance, but *facilitate* it.
- Team Developer: EPMs are intentional about developing the team. They realize it doesn't just happen, it requires thought, effort and an investment of their time.
- Conflict Manager: Properly managed conflict is good for teams – it indicates they care about the project and the work. Channeling that energy makes the difference between negative and positive outcomes.
- Accountability Coach: In these days of "Do More With Less" we need EPMs who know how to balance empowerment with accountability in order to facilitate self-directed and well managed workgroups.

How will you know when you've crossed over and become an Extreme Project Manager? For me it was when I actually started enjoying the job instead of just putting in time. And what made the job enjoyable was when the team was enjoying it, too. The quality of our deliverables was top-notch, our reputations and credibility improved and I stopped fighting the revolving door of human resources. If you're trying to figure out exactly *how* Extreme you are – where you are on the Extreme scale – here's some things you may consider:
- Assess your leadership skills: Ask others – those who have observed you, those who report to you, past team members. People are happy to give you feedback! If possible, ask your Human Resources department to conduct a 360° review on you. This

encapsulates the feedback from your superiors, peers and subordinates to give you a good 360° view of your leadership competencies. You might also consider finding a coach – a trusted advisor who will give you honest input.
- Review your team development process: Have you done all the steps we've discussed – are there basic ground rules documented? Does the team understand the project goals? Look around at your team members in the next meeting and honestly assess how much you *really know about each one of them*.
- Evaluate the level of conflict occurring between your team members. Ask yourself why it might be happening and what you should be doing to manage it better. Remember that conflict is a necessary ingredient to effective, collaborative, creative problem solving, but it's your job to properly manage it.
- Assess how accountable your team members appear to be and determine how empowered you have allowed them to be. Peer-to-peer accountability is a strong motivator – ask the team how well they think you (and they!) are doing in this area.

Regardless of what you may have thought in the past, project management equals people management. Period. End of story. As a project manager, exercise control in the area where it will matter most – how our team members interact with one another. When a group of *individuals* finally become a *team*, the odds greatly increase in your favor. Creating a cohesive, gelled unit, working in community to achieve a common goal is the surest guarantee of success that I've found!

One last piece of wisdom and advice? Lighten up! No one gets out of this life alive! Manage the people side of things and THEY will help you manage the rest!

Appendix

I've consolidated a few of my favorite exercises, tricks, and ideas to help get you started. Feel free to steal, edit, expand upon or otherwise modify but please, use your freedom with discretion. Whenever in doubt, check with your Human Resources department before implementing any of my suggestions. I assume no responsibility for how well *my* techniques fit into *your* culture! If you *do* try some, I'd love to hear about your experience!

Fun (at least I think so!) Activities

Outside Inside Exercise

Objective:
Helps team members get to know one another better as well as encourages the team members to "reward" one another and facilitates trust.

Instructions:
1. Go around the table and each member tells one another what is the biggest strength that they (the hearer) bring to the project. For example, Bob tells Anne, Mary, Steve and Joe what unique strength each of them brings. Then Anne tells Bob, Mary, Steve and Joe, and so forth. (If the team is very large, break into smaller groups of no more than 5.)
2. Go around the table again and each member confesses about themselves what strength they feel they are holding back on.
3. **(For mature teams)** Each member indicates an area of weakness that they would like the team to help them improve upon.

Reconvene and facilitate a debriefing discussion.

How to Make a Great Peanut Butter and Jelly Sandwich

Objective:
To demonstrate how unclear our communication can sometimes be.

Supplies:
Loaf of bread
Jar of peanut butter
Jar of jelly
Knife

Players:
Select two people, one director and one do-er, give instructions to each of them, without each one seeing the other's instructions. (It helps if the do-er has a good personality!)

Instructions to the Do-ers
Follow the director's directions to the letter.
Assume nothing. Do only what he or she tells you.
Examples:
- If he or she does not tell you to take 2 slices of bread out of the package, use the whole loaf in the package.
- If he or she does not say to *spread* the jam or peanut butter on the bread, put the *jar* on the bread.
- If he or she doesn't say use a knife, don't.
- If he or she doesn't specify how much jam or peanut butter to put on the knife, use as much as you can possibly scoop out.

- If he or she doesn't tell you to clean the knife between uses, don't.

Instructions to the Directors:
Provide the do-er with verbal instructions for how to make a peanut butter and jelly sandwich.

Debrief the team members after the exercise.

EXTREME Project Manager Makeover!

Management Speak Bingo

Objective:
Alleviate stress and build camaraderie.

Directions:
Before a project review meeting where a lot of people will be in attendance, create some bingo cards with typical management-speak or buzzwords, such as:
- "Thinking outside the box"
- "Drill down"
- "Synergy"
- "Recursive thinking"
- "I've got that on my radar"
- "Low-hanging fruit"
- "Coopetition"
- ...Etc, etc, you get the idea

Pass these out to your team and tell them to play surreptitiously. Winning is the same as in regular Bingo – filling the spots down, across or diagonally. If they win, they should give a signal, such as cough or sneeze. Later on, reward the winners with some silly prize. ***This game should definitely be played with discretion – but it can alleviate a lot of stress during difficult times and increase camaraderie among your team members.***

Constant Change

Objective:
To illustrate how change can impact our progress and how to apply good teamwork and maintain unity to overcome the challenges.

Instructions:
Break into teams and give each team a puzzle to assemble – the more difficult, the better, as they will never actually finish the puzzle. The teams are not competing against one another

Some team members have been given specific roles to play but the others do not know this. The roles, and what they will typically be saying:

> **Negative Nancy:** It isn't going to work. I hate this project. I wish I could work with the other team, etc.
> **Izzy Idea:** (Constantly makes suggestions that are useless or derailing.) Maybe we should start all over. What if we turned it upside down?
> **Roger Rah-Rah:** (Constant patter of positive energy – not much help, though.) We can do it! We're so great! We're the best!
> **Strategic Sally:** Let's slow down a minute and look at the instructions. Maybe Joe should read the instructions aloud while we follow.

While the teams are trying to assemble the puzzle, the facilitator (acting in the role of management or sponsor) interrupts from time to time:

- Takes members from one team and puts them on another
- Changes the time requirements
- Interrupts and asks for a status check or asks mundane questions
- Takes some puzzle pieces away

(The facilitator cannot help the team members – if they ask how they should proceed after he or she has taken away puzzle pieces, just shrug)

The exercise should take about 15 minutes. When time is up, debrief the team. Have the role players reveal themselves and discuss which challenges proved the most upsetting, disruptive or annoying. Ask which roles helped progress and which ones hurt and discuss how the game applies to their normal work situations. *I've used difficult Lego-type models with this exercise as well as complex puzzles.*

SABOTAGE!

Objective:
To build teams and start discussions about trust.

Order of Cards: ♦ ♥ ♣ ♠
Two through Ace
Face up (two of diamonds on top of stack)
No jokers

Directions:
Divide into teams of 4-5 people and give each team a deck of shuffled cards. Their assignment is to arrange the cards in the correct order and give the deck to the facilitator. If the arrangement is correct, the team will receive a point, and another shuffled deck for processing. The team with the highest number of points at the end of a five-minute period wins.

Note: Some teams (but not all!) will have a **saboteur** in their midst who will try to reduce team productivity. During the process, the saboteur may make inappropriate suggestions, ask irrelevant questions, try to confuse and irritate others, slow down the process, lose a card, or misplace a card. The saboteur tries to work in a sneaky fashion – if their team members catch them, their team forfeits.

This exercise is great for team-building and starting discussions about trust. Many of the teams will *assume* they have a saboteur and not trust one another.

Speaking The Same Language?

Objective:
A fun exercise to start serious discussions about our personal motivation, possible hidden agendas and communication effectiveness.

Scenario: Two people are talking. One is describing their vacation experience with great enthusiasm and vigor, however, he or she is using a *made up* language that the audience cannot understand. The second person is charged with interpreting the message for the audience.

Instructions for Person One: You must use lots of enthusiasm and hand motions or other means of describing what you are saying. It is vital that your message gets through to your audience.

Instructions for Person Two: You must interpret with authority and certainty. Completely disregard what the other person appears to be trying to communicate and tell the story that *you* choose to tell.

Icebreaker – You'll Never Guess

Each person writes on a piece of paper something about themselves that the rest of the team probably doesn't know. The facilitator collects the papers and then reads them out loud while the team tries to guess who is who.

Outrageous Motivators

Meeting Improvements and Team Activities
- Pass out to all attendees plastic hand-clappers – you can get them for $1 at party stores. Use them to reward good thinking, new ideas, accomplishments, solutions.
- Hold your meetings somewhere totally unexpected: outside in the parking lot, in a nearby park, in the company gym. Get creative!
- Invite customers to focus meetings with the team members. It encourages information sharing and cross-functional cooperation.
- For lengthy or tedious brainstorming sessions, be sure to include food. Changing the locale for this, too, can help facilitate problem solving and generate ideas.
- Include a short time for some fun – someone tells a funny joke or story, give out a silly award, or some other boredom reliever. Doesn't have to take a lot of time but makes a meeting more bearable.
- Start your meeting with **Your Biggest Failure or Faux Pas**. Anyone can share what was the dumbest thing they've ever done or possibly what was the most ridiculous thing that happened on the project in the last week or so. This needs to be a no-harm, no-foul kind of confession – no one is going to get in trouble for what they share. This exercise encourages risk taking and builds camaraderie.
- Before a meeting, pass out "Red Cards" to your team members. If the discussion goes "off-track" anyone can raise the Red Card to being things back around.

Rewards and Recognition

- Have a team item that becomes a regular award. One of my teams had a Xena (the warrior princess!) doll that we used as a bi-weekly trophy. The team member that performed well during that period (as determined by the previous winner) was awarded Xena. As time went on, Xena took on a new look and identity as she made the rounds of the team members – she had some tattoos drawn on her, her hair was often braided, she changed clothes, etc. One time she was awarded to a member who had just returned from maternity leave and Xena was carrying a baby on her back!

  This tradition took on an interesting life, though, when the team voted to award Xena to our very proper, buttoned-up CEO for something *he* had accomplished. I was a good sport and delivered her to him, along with an explanation of why he was being so honored, and he was very touched! So much so, that I had to ask his Executive Assistant to give her back to us after a few months had gone by!
- Select a theme for your project and create items that reflect that theme. For example, one of my clients used the metaphor of a crew team to represent their commitment to good team work. The item they selected to use as an icon was a rowing oar. They even took to scratching notes and sayings in the wood before awarding it to one another. You might have posters or notepads made to reflect your theme.
- Tell your team members that if they complete _____ you will call their mother and tell her how great they are! Be sure you follow through!

- Conduct a "Most Likely To..." contest about the members of the team. Distribute a survey with various criteria on it:
  "Most likely to have ten kids"
  "Most likely to win Miss Congeniality"
  "Most likely to spend a night in jail"
  "Most likely to become a millionaire"
  ...etc, etc
  Share the findings at a team meeting or other gathering.
- Adopt the "U Rock" recognition process. One of my clients actually had a rock that they had labeled "U ROCK!" in bright red paint and they awarded it to team members or other supporters. I had cards printed that said "U Rock!" with a place to write a note to the recipient. I passed these out freely to employees, co-workers, cross-functional peers, etc. People love the recognition!
- Have an awards ceremony at a local brewery or restaurant but not a *typical* awards ceremony! Make the award something meaningful to the recipient or to the project. For example, on one of my software projects, the engineers had been in "Documentation Hell" for two months – they had not been able to write any code while they were documenting requirements and creating design documents. I "awarded" them each a foot-tall evergreen tree because they had been "Killing trees!" Another engineer and his business analyst had been chartered with reducing the time it took for a particular process to run. They were both awarded a toy Shaving Kit because they had "shaved" time off the process!

- Reward your business partners and customers – show them how much you appreciate their cooperation and support. I mentioned the Thanksgiving ritual earlier in the book, where we made huge platters of goodies and treats and delivered them to gatekeepers and customers to acknowledge their contribution to our success – this works for any business partner you want to encourage. Your reward could be baked goods or candy – get creative! If you have time and money, cook breakfast for them!

Gallows Humor
(Very motivating and great for building camaraderie – <u>use your discretion and wisdom!</u>)
- Host a party at the end of a project called the "What Were We Thinking?" party. This is especially effective if the project was difficult (short schedule, changing scope, etc). Invite your sponsors and customers to share in the fun.
- Stage a Survivor Party with trials and immunity challenges associated with different project objectives. Be sure to include voting someone off at different points in the game.

Motivators
- Getting the group together for a happy hour after work is a great motivator. Don't try to institute a "no work discussions" policy because it won't work, but having some of those discussions off site in a relaxed atmosphere does wonders for team building.
- Take a team member to management meetings with you. It helps expand their view of what is going on,

demonstrates their value to others and helps them see that you value their view and input.
- Spend time with them both one-on-one and in groups of two or three. Take them to lunch, get to know them better. Ask for their ideas and insights on the project.
- Let your team members manage certain parts of the project based on their areas of interest. Encourage them to implement ideas of their own, such as a project newsletter or a team website or wiki.
- Involve your team in decision making and problem solving. This validates their expertise and place on the team.
- If your training budget is limited, send as many as you can and have them conduct a training session for the other members.
- Have candy on your desk! I always had a bucket of chocolate (and it has to be the good stuff!) on my desk. It encouraged team members to stop in and kept them full and happy!
- Don't limit your training to only technical or skills training. Try to incorporate some kind of culture or motivational training, as well.
- Give out little gifts for no reason at all –just because you are so lucky to have a team like this one! These can be post-it notes, Starbucks cards, food items, etc. Keep your eyes open for special $1 sales and stock up.
- Have T-shirts made with your project or team name on them.
- Do something "theme" related. For example, we had a team discussion about Pike Place Fish Market and how their culture impacted their service delivery. We followed the discussion with a luncheon that had to

incorporate fish in some way. It was an *interesting* potluck and a lot of fun!
- Along the theme idea: have the usual Hawaiian Shirt day or something similar. Some people really like this idea and get pretty creative. For example, one project team I know decided to dress like the CFO for Halloween. He was the project sponsor and a great sport so they all took on different "characters": one was "Sleepy Alex" and wore pajamas; another was "Corporate Alex" and dressed in a 3 piece suit and so forth. They all wore black-rimmed eyeglasses like his and, because he *always wore a tie*, they all included ties in their costumes! Great fun!

Stress Relievers
- Have small toys all over the department. If your organization doesn't have a basketball hoop in the parking lot, install one of those little Nerf ones. I gave one of my teams a huge plastic tub full of little dollar toys – squirt guns, play-doh, puzzles, etc. They loved it!
- Give your customer a toy dart board with your team's picture on it – share the laugh! Or give your team a dart board with *your* picture on it!
- Put up a dry-erase board in the war room, hallway, cubicle center, etc, and start a "discussion". Ask a question and let the team members write to their heart's content. The question doesn't have to be project related – it can be philosophical (avoid controversial subjects!) or humorous. Change the "discussion" weekly.
- When your team starts doing crazy things on their own, you know you've hit the jackpot. On one of my

teams, two of the members took all of us out to the parking lot at the end of our regular status meeting. Hanging from a tree was a *Sponge Bob piñata*. We all became six-years old again and took turns breaking the piñata as amazing things fell out. In addition to the usual candy, there were also small bottles of alcohol, a stapler, someone's shoe, a full box of red licorice, a can of Vienna sausage, a box of q-tips, etc, etc. The whole exercise only took about 15 minutes but gained *hours* of camaraderie and productivity from the team!

- Call a Chinese Fire Drill in the cubicles. Blow a whistle and get everyone to stop what they're doing, run around the work area and return to their cubes. (Be sure you do this at a time when they could actually participate – not when they're all on the phone with a customer!)

It's not the money!

I hope you get one or two ideas from some of these crazy, but highly effective, tips! Before you discount my approach, though, by claiming to have no budget, let me give you some tips. **The Dollar Store is your friend.** If you use some creativity and time, you can spend less than $20 to pull together a stellar awards ceremony or motivating gifts. I also used to search the *Successories-type* websites for close-out items and stocked up. When the team goes out for a Happy Hour, it's Dutch treat – having to pay their own way doesn't diminish the value at all and makes it even more special on the rare occasion when you *can* pick up the tab. It isn't the gift you give or the money you spend, it's the time you put into it and the recognition they receive. *I cannot stress enough how important it is to show others how much you value their contributions!*

Investment: Time, energy, minimal $$
Return on Investment: PRICELESS!

I would love to hear from you, Extreme Project Manager!
Please write me at:
pattie@thevargasgroup.net
www.thevargasgroup.net

About Pattie Vargas

Pattie Vargas, Principal and founder of **The Vargas Group**, is uniquely qualified to assist organizations in achieving dramatic improvements in workplace performance. An expert in classical process improvement and technical project management, she provides the critical missing piece to many failed initiatives: effective business relationships. Her specialty in interpersonal skills and career development for technical disciplines assists her clients in aligning their people and processes, resulting in increased commitment, accountability and results. She partners with senior leaders to develop solutions and customize programs for each client environment.

Pattie's qualifications include more than 20 years of team and project management, human performance improvement, organizational development and interpersonal skills development. She has a Masters degree in Organizational Management and a Bachelors degree in Business Management. She holds the coveted Project Management Professional (PMP) certification from the Project Management Institute as well as a certification in Total Quality Management and Process Improvement from the University of California, San Diego. She is certified in the DISC Behavioral Assessments.

Pattie is a frequent conference speaker on the topics of inter-personal business relationships, with a particular emphasis on soft skills development for technical disciplines. Pattie has developed and delivered successful programs that address issues with employee retention, management development and team effectiveness. She partners with organizational leaders to deliver coaching and training programs unique to their corporate culture and organizational maturity. Her teambuilding methodology was featured in an edition of PMNetwork magazine. She was named one of the Top 10 Business Women of 2007 by The American Business Women's Association and serves as one of their National Ambassadors.

www.ingramcontent.com/pod-product-compliance
Lightning Source LLC
Chambersburg PA
CBHW030807180526
45163CB00003B/1177